LIVING THE ETHICS AND
MORALITY OF ISLAM

HOW TO LIVE AS A MUSLIM SERIES

LIVING THE ETHICS AND
MORALITY OF ISLAM

Ali Ünal

TUGHRA
BOOKS
New Jersey

Published by Tughra Books

345 Clifton Ave.,

Clifton, NJ, 07011,

USA

www.tughrabooks.com

Library of Congress Cataloging-in-Publication Data Available

ISBN: 978-1-59784-212-9

CONTENTS

INTRODUCTION

T he first volume of this series lays out and explains the elements of *aqida*, or faith, which are essential for Muslims. The second volume deals with the five pillars of Islam, the obligatory acts of worship and their conditions as well as the issues of family life and the lawful and the unlawful based on the Qur'an and Sunna; in short, the daily life of a Muslim. This third and final volume lays out guidelines for our conduct towards Allah, towards our selves, and towards others in our daily life; that is, being the living embodiment of Islam.

To be a Muslim means more than knowing some elements of theology, or fasting, praying and performing pilgrimage in accordance with the rules. These elements of the Religion must never be neglected or abandoned; they are essential and obligatory. However, in addition, we are confronted with the task of bringing our behavior into harmony with the universe and with the original Divine pattern that Allah the Most Merciful, the Most Compassionate created. We must do this without falling into the trap of confusing our *nafs al-ammarat*, our evil-commanding soul, with our *fitrah*, or being perfect humans.

With our human tendency to think well of ourselves, which can lead to self-flattery and self-deceit, how can we truly distinguish between the pull of our God-given nature and the impulses of our carnal soul?

We must arrange our individual, family, and social life in conformity with Allah's Will by living our lives in accord with the Holy Qur'an, which was sent down as the Guide and the Criterion.

Also, we must follow the perfect example of conduct that Allah in His mercy has placed before us. The one who best embodies perfect harmony between religious principle and self-conduct is Prophet Muhammad, peace and blessings be upon him. Allah gave the Prophet perfect character, and commanded him to teach the same character or ethics to his followers. The words and deeds of the Messenger of Allah, peace and blessings be upon him, are recorded in the *hadith*, and the scholars have therefore drawn guidance from the *hadith* as well as the Qur'an for the conduct of Muslims in matters great and small.

In this respected tradition, this volume is intended to lay out detailed and helpful guidelines to be followed conscientiously by all those who wish to perfect their character and imitate Allah's Messenger, peace and blessings be upon him, in word and deed as commanded in the Holy Qur'an.

CHAPTER 1

Islamic Morality

ISLAMIC MORALITY

The term "Islamic morality" can, in one respect, be defined or summed up as "perfectibility of humanity." Prophet Muhammad, upon him be peace and blessings, declared, "I have been sent to perfect the standards and beauties of good morals."[1] When asked which believer was the best on account of his or her belief, he answered, "The one who is the best in character."[2] Anas ibn Malik, may Allah be pleased with him, narrated:

> The Prophet, upon him be peace and blessings, was the best among the people (both in shape and character) and was the most generous of them, and was the bravest of them. Once, during the night, the people of Medina got afraid (of a sound). So the people went towards that sound, but the Prophet, upon him be peace and blessings, having gone to that sound before them, met them, saying, "Don't be afraid, don't be afraid." (At that time) he was riding a horse belonging to Abu Talha and it was unsaddled, and he was carrying a sword slung at his neck. The Prophet said, "I found it (the horse running swiftly and comfortably) like a sea, or, it is the sea indeed."[3]

This is natural, because Allah praises and consoles His most distinguished servant Prophet Muhammad, upon him be peace and blessings, not with His extraordinary favors but with his laudable virtues and praiseworthy qualities, declaring, *"You are surely of a sublime character, and do act by a sublime pattern of conduct"* (68:4). His nature was the aim and fruit of his creation. Since the Prophet's conduct embodied Islam and the Qur'an, when his wife 'A'isha, may Allah be pleased with her, was asked about his conduct by Sa'id ibn Hisham, she answered, "Do you not read the Qur'an? His conduct is (the embodiment of) the Qur'an."[4]

Prophet Muhammad, upon him be peace and blessings, frequently encouraged good morals and warned against having an evil character. For example, he declared, "There are two characteristics which cannot be found in a believer: niggardliness and bad morals."[5] He also said that by his good character a believer would attain the degree of one who prays during the night and fasts during the day.[6] He also said, "There is nothing heavier than good character put in the scale of a believer on the Day of Resurrection."[7]

The two concepts which are generally used for good morals and virtuousness are *khuluq* (good nature) and *adab* (mannerliness). Fethullah Gülen writes about *khuluq* as follows:

> *Khuluq* (good nature), in addition to meaning temperament, disposition, and character, is a goal to which a traveler to Allah aspires, for it is the most important dimension of creation. In brief, this station means that one is characterized (equipped) with Allah's way of acting. For example, Allah is All-Forgiving; therefore, one must be forgiving. One who realizes this sacred goal can easily perform all good acts or deeds.
>
> The words *khalq* (creation) and *khuluq* (nature) are derived from the same root word. *Khalq* relates to the external form or appearance, the visible, material, and experienced dimension of existence; *khuluq* is concerned with the spiritual dimension, meaning, or content. An individual cannot be judged or known by his or her outer appearance, for one's real identity lies in one's character, temperament, and natural disposition. No matter how many different images one may project, one's true character or temperament will eventually reveal itself. How meaningful are the following words of an Arab poet of the pre-Islamic Age of Ignorance:
>
>> If a man has a bad quality, sooner or later it will reveal itself;
>> Let him continue to think that it can remain hidden.
>
> In other words, the outer appearance is deceiving, for one's natural disposition removes or corrects all deceptions and thereby reveals one's true nature. Since one may acquire a second nature through education and habituation, moralists divide nature into good and bad. In the present context, we use "nature" to mean "good nature."

The most accurate standard of a good spiritual life is good nature. One who has taken a few steps forward in good nature may be regarded as advanced in the spiritual life. Although the wonders worked, dazzling stations, and "superhuman" actions may be acceptable when they issue from good nature, they are worthless if not combined with good nature.

The indications of having a good nature have been summarized as follows: a person possessing this quality does not hurt anybody by either word or deed, pardons those who hurt him or her and forgives the evils done, and reciprocates evil with good.... Many people seem to be good natured, mild-mannered, and humane, although their good conduct and mildness are no more than affectations. When they experience a little irritation, anger, or harsh treatment, their true nature is revealed. One who has a good nature does not change his or her manners even when in a hellish state, but remains mild and shows no harshness. A heart open to good nature is like a very broad space to bury one's anger and rage. Those intolerant and impatient ones who display bad conduct can find no place to bury their anger, hatred, and ill feelings.

Let us conclude this discussion with the following couplet:

It is by good nature that a man can be perfected;
It is by good nature that the order of the world is maintained.[8]

What follows is a summary of what Fethullah Gülen writes about *adab* (mannerliness):

The meaning of *adab* covers being sensible and reasonable, well-behaved, well-mannered, treating people kindly. It is also used to defend against errors and to distinguish the factors leading to errors. It is dealt with under the categories of "mannerliness in *Shari'a*," "mannerliness in serving Allah's cause," and "mannerliness before Allah, the absolute Truth." Mannerliness in *Shari'a* is knowing the commandments of the Religion and practicing them in daily life. Mannerliness in serving Allah's cause is being ahead of everyone in striving and making efforts but preferring others to oneself in obtaining the fruits, receiving the wages and being appreciated and rewarded for effort. It is also doing all the prerequisites for a desired result but attributing all good and comeliness and success to Allah. As for mannerliness before Allah, it consists of "refining" and "adorning" nearness to Allah, in collectedness and self-possession, avoiding excessive claims and reckless or casual speech or behavior incompatible with the rules of the Islamic Law.

Another approach to mannerliness is dealing with it under the categories of "mannerliness in *Shari'a* or rules," "mannerliness in spiritual education or journeying," "mannerliness in knowledge of Allah," and "mannerliness in attainment of truth." The first means practicing the Sunna (the way) of Allah's Messenger, upon him be peace and blessings, in all his acts, sayings, and approvals. The second means, together with submission to and love of him, serving the spiritual guide, and attending his discourses. The third consists of preserving the balance between nearness to Allah and self-possession, between fear and hope or expectation, and awareness of self-poverty and impotence in the face of the Divine favors coming directly from Allah. As for the fourth, it is perfect attachment to Allah in complete detachment from everything other than Him, without having any expectation other than obtaining His approval and good pleasure.

In one respect, spiritual education in Islam consists of "mannerliness"; it consists of expressing the good manners proper to each occasion, each spiritual state, and each rank or station. However, only if believers have been able to realize all of these good manners in their own inner world, can they really be well-mannered in their attitudes and ways of behavior. Apparent and superficial manners, such as have not been ingrained in their self and become an essential part of their nature, will mean no more than an outward show and cannot become permanent as habits. Nor are they worth anything in the sight of Allah, Who judges a person by his or her inner world.

According to Abu Nasr at-Tusi,[9] mannerliness can be summarized in the following three paragraphs.

- The mannerliness of literary men who seek beauty and virtue in writing and speech, which some Muslim spiritual guides regard as "gossip" if they do not originate in the heart.
- The mannerliness of those who represent the religion of Islam at the level of a pure spiritual life, which is regarded as consisting of refining the selfhood through disciplines, and the feelings through love and fear of Allah, and in meticulously following the religious commandments.

- The mannerliness of those who through continuous self-control and introspection maintain the purity of heart at the level of neither imagining or conceiving of anything contrary to the awareness of always being in the presence of Allah and overseen by Him.

Those who have been able to attain the truth have attached much importance to all kinds of mannerliness and tried their hardest to make it an essential, ingrained part of their human nature. They have many wise sayings uttered in this respect, of which they have themselves striven to be the embodiments in utmost sincerity. To cite a few examples:

The following is a jewel-like saying quoted from Imam 'Ali, the cousin of the Prophet, upon him be peace and blessings:

Nowadays misfortunes are common, which is not to be wondered at.
What is to be wondered at is how one could remain upright and maintain one's integrity among so many misfortunes.
Beauty is not that which the garment one wears adds to him.
Rather, it is the beauty of knowledge and mannerliness.

In addition to what we have already said concerning the practical aspect of mannerliness or being well-mannered in behavior, the following reflections are worth recalling:

It is mannerliness which a person should always wear:
Without good manners, one is as if naked.

Mannerliness is to be found in the people of knowledge.
A student without good manners cannot be a learned one.

The order of the world is through mannerliness;
Again, through mannerliness is human perfection.

Expressive of purity in thought, uprightness in the heart, and a deep relationship with Allah, mannerliness in speech has been stressed for centuries in all schools which concern themselves with moral and religious education or with spiritual training. Wahbi says:

Do not open your mouth for idle talk, be well-mannered in speech.
Take care of what you may say so that afterwards you do not become uneasy.

Another voices his thought about mannerliness as follows:

Mannerliness is a crown from the light of Allah:
Wear that crown and be safe from every misfortune.

Two Perspectives on a Muslim's Life

In respect of Islamic morality and being equipped with good morals, we can view a Muslim's life from two perspectives: one concerns a Muslim's individual perfectibility, and the other their relationships with their Creator, their own selves, and their environment, including the natural environment. In other words, an Islamic view of life concerns the knowledge, discipline, and science of humankind's rights and obligations and of what is good and bad for humankind on the individual and collective levels. Thus a Muslim's life consists of a set of rules, rights and obligations by which he or she is expected to live. Broadly speaking, Islamic law deals with our life in terms of our relationship with our Creator, ourselves (the rights of our soul on us, that is, our duties towards ourselves), other people, and our natural environment (the rights of the resources that Allah has given to us for our benefit).

The Prophet, upon him be peace and blessings, established a bond of brotherhood between Salman and Abu'd-Darda'. Salman paid a visit to Abu'd-Darda and found Ummu'-Darda' (Abu'd-Darda's wife) dressed in shabby clothes and asked her why she was in that state. She replied, "Your brother, Abu'd-Darda' has nothing to do with this world." In the meantime Abu'd-Darda' came and prepared a meal for Salman, and said to him, "Please, eat for I am fasting." Salman said, "I am not going to eat unless you eat." So Abu'd-Darda' ate. When it was night, Abu'd-Darda' got up for the *tahajjud* Prayer. Salman said to him, "Sleep," and he slept. Again Abu'd-Darda' got up for the Prayer, and Salman said to him, "Sleep." When it was the last part of the night, Salman said to him, "Get up now for the Prayer." So both of them offered their *tahajjud* Prayers and Salman said to Abu'd-Darda', "Your Lord has a right on you; and your soul has a right on you; and your family has a right on you; so you should give the rights of all those who have a right on you." Later on Abu'd-Darda' visited the Prophet, upon him be peace and blessings, and mentioned that to him. The Prophet, said, "Salman has spoken the truth."[11]

Our Duties towards Allah Almighty and His Messenger

We are first dutiful towards Allah, our Creator and Nourisher, and Allah's Messenger, upon him be peace and blessings. We must believe in Allah without associating any partners with Him, obey Him in all His injunctions and prohibitions with sincerity, feel utmost respect for and awe of Him, love and fear Him and love or dislike others on account of His love, act in awareness that He always sees us, and be pleased with or show resignation to whatever He decrees concerning us.

As for our duties towards Allah's Messenger, upon him be peace and blessings, we must believe in him as a Prophet and Messenger of Allah and in whatever he conveyed to us in the name of the Religion. We must prefer him to our own selves and his demands and judgments to our own wishes and views. We must be respectful for him, and love him sincerely. We invoke Allah's blessings and peace upon him and his household when his name is mentioned. We must be very careful not to do and say anything which implies disrespect for him. The Qur'an declares:

قُلْ إِنْ كَانَ آبَاؤُكُمْ وَأَبْنَاؤُكُمْ وَإِخْوَانُكُمْ وَأَزْوَاجُكُمْ وَعَشِيرَتُكُمْ وَأَمْوَالٌ اقْتَرَفْتُمُوهَا وَتِجَارَةٌ تَخْشَوْنَ كَسَادَهَا وَمَسَاكِنُ تَرْضَوْنَهَا أَحَبَّ إِلَيْكُمْ مِنَ اللهِ وَرَسُولِهِ وَجِهَادٍ فِي سَبِيلِهِ فَتَرَبَّصُوا حَتَّى يَأْتِيَ اللهُ بِأَمْرِهِ وَاللهُ لَا يَهْدِي الْقَوْمَ الْفَاسِقِينَ

Say: "If your fathers, and your children, and your brothers and sisters, and your spouses, and your kindred vvand clan, and the wealth you have acquired, and the commerce you fear may slacken, and the dwellings that you love to live in, are dearer to you than Allah and His Messenger and striving in His cause, then wait until Allah brings about His decree. Allah does not guide the transgressing people (who prefer worldly things to

Him, His Messenger and striving in His cause, to truth and true happiness in both the world and the Hereafter). (9:24)

The Prophet has a higher claim on the believers than they have on their own selves, and (seeing that he is as a father to them) his wives are (as) their mothers. (33:6)

Whoever defies Allah and His Messenger, (let everyone know that) Allah is severe in retribution. (8:13)

Keep from disobedience to Allah in reverence for Him and piety, and set things right among yourselves to allow no discord; and obey Allah and His Messenger if you are true believers. (8:1)

You never find a people who truly believe in Allah and the Last Day loving toward those who oppose Allah and His Messenger, even if they be their (own) parents, or their children, or their brothers (and sisters), or their clan. Those (are they) in whose hearts Allah has inscribed faith and has strengthened them with a spirit from Him (which is the source of their spiritual vigor and intellectual enlightenment). And He will admit them into Gardens through which rivers flow, therein to abide. Allah is well-pleased with them, and they are well-pleased with Him. Those are the party of Allah. Be aware: the party of Allah are those who are the prosperous. (58:22)

Indeed, you have had an excellent example to follow in Abraham and those in his company, when they said to their (idolatrous) people (who were their kin): "We are quit of you and whatever you worship besides Allah. We have rejected you (in your polytheism), and there has arisen between us and you enmity and hate forever until you believe in Allah alone (as the only One to be worshipped." (So it was) except for Abraham's saying to his father: "I most surely will plead for Allah's forgiveness for you, though I have no power at all to do anything for you against Allah." (And their prayer was:) "O Our Lord! It is in You that We have put our trust, and it is to You that we turn in utmost sincerity and devotion; and to You is the homecoming." (60:4)

O you who believe! Do not be forward in the Presence of Allah and His Messenger. Keep from disobedience to Allah in piety and reverence for Him, so that you may deserve His protection.

Surely Allah is All-Hearing, All-Knowing. O you who believe! Do not raise your voices above the voice of the Prophet, nor speak loudly when addressing him, as you would speak loudly to one another, lest your good deeds go in vain without your perceiving it. Those who lower their voices in the presence of Allah's Messenger, those are they whose hearts Allah has tested and proven for piety and reverence for Him. For them there is forgiveness (to bring unforeseen rewards) and a tremendous reward. Those who call out to you from behind the private apartments (which you share with your wives), most of them do not reason and understand (and are, therefore, lacking in good manners). If (instead of shouting to you to come out to them) they had been patient until you came out to them, it would certainly have been better for them (in respect of the manners due to you from them). However, Allah is All-Forgiving, All-Compassionate (especially towards His believing servants, and may forgive ill-manners arising from ignorance). (49:1–5)

Those who affront Allah and His Messenger (through disrespect for Him in words and acts and for His Messenger and Islamic values), Allah certainly curses them (excludes them from His mercy) in this world and the Hereafter, and He has prepared for them a shameful, humiliating punishment. (33:57)

Do not treat the Messenger's summoning and praying for you as your summoning and praying for one another. Indeed, Allah knows well those of you who surreptitiously sneak away, taking cover behind one another. So, let those who go against the Messenger's order beware, lest a bitter trial befall them or a painful punishment afflict them. (24:63)

Surely Allah and His angels bless the Prophet (He always treats him with His special mercy, with the angels praying to Him to grant him the highest station of praise with Him, and for the decisive victory of his Religion). O you who believe, invoke the blessings of Allah on him, and pray to Allah to bestow His peace on him, greeting him with the best greeting. (Love and follow him with utmost sincerity and faithfulness, and give yourselves to his way with perfect submission). (33:56)

We must be very careful about carrying out the orders of Allah and His Messenger, and observing the bounds set by Allah. Obeying Allah and His Messenger and observing the bounds set by Allah is the guarantee of preserving unity among us, and fulfilling Divine commandments lightens our burden. The Qur'an declares:

> And obey Allah and His Messenger, and do not dispute with one another, or else you may lose heart and your power and energy desert you; and remain steadfast. Surely Allah is with those who remain steadfast. (8:46)

> These are the bounds set by Allah. Whoever obeys Allah and His Messenger (by remaining within these bounds), Allah will admit him into Gardens through which rivers flow, abiding therein. That is the supreme triumph. But whoever disobeys Allah and His Messenger and exceeds His bounds, Allah will admit him into a Fire, to abide therein, and for him is a shameful, humiliating punishment. (4:13–14)

> Allah wills to turn to you (with mercy and favor by explaining to you His commandments and guiding you to the Straight Path), whereas those who follow (their) lusts (for women, offspring, wealth, fame, status, and position) desire you to deviate greatly (from the Straight Path). Allah wills to lighten for you (your burdens), for human has been created weak (liable to err). (4:27–28)

As Muslims, we must wholeheartedly accept or resign ourselves to any judgment given by Allah's Messenger, upon him be peace and blessings, or by a Muslim authority judging according to the Qur'an and the Sunna:

> By your Lord, they do not (truly) believe unless they make you (O Messenger) the judge regarding any dispute between them, and then find not the least vexation within themselves over what you have decided, and surrender in full submission. (4:65)

We must refrain from slandering Allah by fabricating anything and attributing it to Him and denying His Revelation and signs:

Who is more in wrong than he who fabricates falsehood in attribution to Allah and denies His Revelations and signs (in the universe and their selves)? Their full portion of Allah's decree (concerning life and providence) will reach them, until Our envoys (angels assigned for this duty) come to them to take their souls, and say: "Where, now, are those beings whom you have deified and invoked apart from Allah?" They say: "They have failed us," and thus bear witness against themselves that they were (always) unbelievers. (7:37)

We must also refrain from saying things about Allah and the religion about which we have no sure knowledge:

Say: "My Lord has made unlawful only indecent, shameful deeds (like fornication, adultery, prostitution, and homosexuality), whether those of them that are apparent and committed openly or those that are committed secretly; and any act explicitly sinful; and insolence and offenses (against the Religion, life, personal property, others' chastity, and mental and bodily health), which is openly unjustified; and (it is also forbidden) that you associate partners with Allah, for which He has sent no authority at all, and that you speak against Allah the things about which you have no sure knowledge. (7:33)

Another point to note concerning our duties to Allah and His Messenger is that we cannot count our being Muslims as a favor to them. The Qur'an declares:

They impress it on you as their favor to you that they have submitted (to the rule of Islam and thereby put you under an obligation to them). Say: "Do not count your being Muslims as a favor to me (nor seek to put me under an obligation. The Religion does not belong to me, but to Allah only). It is indeed Allah Who has conferred a favor upon you inasmuch as He has shown you the way to faith—if you are truthful (in your profession of being Muslims, those who have submitted to Allah)." (49:17)

Our Duties towards Our Souls

Each person has some duties towards his or her own soul. Some of these pertain to the body, and some to the intellect and the spirit. We may summarize these duties as follows:

- Training the body. For everyone, it is crucial to keep the body healthy and strong, as well as maintaining its cleanliness. According to a narration of the Prophet, upon him be peace and blessings, "A strong and vigorous believer is better and more lovable to Allah than a frail and weak one."[12]
- Strengthening willpower and avoiding and preserving the body from what is harmful to it.
- Caring for one's health. Health is a great blessing; therefore, it is vital to avoid things that damage health, and to seek treatment when one is ill.
- Refraining from dangerous mortification practices.
- Some of the important duties relating to the mind and intellect are to pursue learning and enlightenment, to awaken higher emotions and positive feelings in the heart, and
- Purifying the soul of sins, refining the "heart", and having a spiritual education.

Family Duties

Family life is the cornerstone of a society. The foundation of a family begins with a husband and wife, and their children. There are special duties owed to these members of one's family.

1. The primary duties of a husband are to behave kindly towards his wife, to meet her basic needs, and maintain and preserve her. Allah's Messenger says, "The most perfect among the believers in respect of faith is the one who is the best of them in character; and the best of you are the kindest towards their wives."[13] Allah always calls the husbands to piety, righteousness, and fear of Allah

in their relations with their wives, and orders them to consort with them in a good manner. For example:

> O you who believe! It is not lawful for you to become inheritors, against their will, of women (of your deceased kinsmen, marrying them against their will, without paying their bridal-due, or forcing them to marry others in return for their bridal-due, as though they were a part of heritable property); nor should you constrain your wives in order to take away anything of what you have given them (as bridal-due or bridal gift), unless they be guilty of indecency in an obvious manner (such as to justify divorce). Consort with them in a good manner, for if you are not pleased with them, it may well be that you dislike something but Allah has set in it much good. (4:19)

The Qur'an describes the marriage contract as a solemn pledge which the women take from the men to honor their rights, and marital relations as the spouses' going in to each other (4:21). In case of discord between spouses and the neglect of marital responsibilities, it advises reconciliation and peaceful settlement:

> If a woman fears from her husband's ill-treatment or (such breach of marital obligations as) his turning away in aversion, then there will be no blame on them to set things right peacefully between them; peaceful settlement is better.... (O husbands) if you do good in consciousness of Allah and act in reverence for Him and piety (in observing the rights of women), then surely Allah is fully aware of what you do. (4:128)

It also encourages the appointment of two arbiters one from among the husband's people and one from among the wife's, and again advises reconciliation (4:35).

As for a wife, her main duties are not to oppose her husband in his proper demands, and to remain loyal to him, and protect his honor and good name, be contented in the family's worldly situation, and avoid waste. The Qur'an declares:

> Good, righteous women are the devoted ones (to Allah) and observant (of their husbands' rights), who guard the secrets

(family honor and property, their chastity, and their husband's rights, especially where there is none to see them, and in the absence of men,) as Allah guards and keeps undisclosed (what should be guarded and private). (4:34)

It is strictly forbidden to instigate spouses against each other. The Prophet, upon him be peace and blessings, said, "If anyone corrupts (instigates) the wife of a man (against him), he [or she] is not from us."[14]

The spouses should help each other with their tasks. Allah's Messenger, upon him be peace and blessings, never refrained from helping his wives at home. Al-Aswad narrates, "I asked 'A'isha what the Prophet, upon him be peace and blessings, used to do at home. She replied, 'He used to keep himself busy serving his family and when it was time for the Prayer, he would get up for the Prayer.'"[15]

2. The basic duties of children towards their parents are as follows: to show them respect and obedience, to always do them good; and avoiding hurting them. A son or daughter who does not look after parents, and show proper respect and obedience to them, or hurts them is a "monstrous" one in the garb of humanity.

When asked who among the people was most deserving of one's good treatment, Allah's Messenger said, "Your mother, again your mother, again your mother, then your father, then your nearest relatives according to the order (of nearness)."[16]

The Qur'an mentions respect for parents and doing them good just after our duty towards Allah Almighty. It declares:

> Your Lord has decreed that you worship none but Him alone, and treat parents with the best of kindness. Should one of them, or both, attain old age in your lifetime, do not say "Ugh!" to them (as an indication of complaint or impatience), nor push them away; and always address them in gracious words. Lower to them the wing of humility out of mercy, and say: "My Lord, have mercy on them even as they cared for me in childhood." Your Lord best knows what is in your souls (in respect of all matters, including what you think of your parents). If you are

righteous (in your thoughts and deeds), then surely He is All-Forgiving to those who turn to Him in humble contrition. (17:23–25)

The only exception to obeying the parents is if they order associating partners with Allah or committing another sin:

> We have enjoined on human in respect with his parents: his mother bore him in strain upon strain, and his weaning was in two years. (So, O human,) be thankful to Me and to your parents. To Me is the final homecoming. But if they strive with you to make you associate with Me something of which you certainly have no knowledge (and which is absolutely contrary to Knowledge), do not obey them. Even then, treat them with kindness and due consideration in respect of (the life of) this world. (31:14–15)

Concerning the importance of observing the rights of parents, Allah's Messenger, upon him be peace and blessings, said, "Allah's good pleasure lies in the parents' being pleased with their children, and so does Allah's wrath lie in the wrath of the parents."[17] He also said, "The parents are a means for entering Paradise through the best of its gates. Either lose that gate by not observing their rights, or try to obtain it by pleasing them."[18]

Duties towards parents do not come to an end when they die. A man came to Allah's Messenger, upon him be peace and blessings, and asked, "Messenger of Allah! Is there any kindness left that I can do for my parents after their death?" He replied, "Yes, you can invoke blessings on them and forgiveness for them, carry out their final instructions after their death, join ties of relationship which are dependent on them, and honor their friends."[19]

We must avoid cursing our parents by cursing the parents of others. Allah's Messenger said, "It is one of the greatest sins that a man should curse his parents." It was asked (by the people), "O Allah's Messenger! How does a man curse his parents?" The Prophet said, "The man abuses the father of another man and the latter abuses the father of the former and abuses his mother."[20]

3. The duties of mothers and fathers towards their children are giving them good, meaningful names, maintaining them during their childhood or during the years when they are unable to earn their lives, and educating them properly.

Fathers and mothers should treat their children equally, holding them in equal regard and affection. They should be models of virtue for them. According to the Qur'an, wealth and children are an adornment of the present, worldly life, but the good, righteous deeds (based on faith and) which endure are better in the sight of the Lord in bringing reward and better to aspire to (18:46). It warns the parents that their worldly possessions and children are but a source of temptation and trial for them, and that Allah is He with Whom there is a tremendous reward (8:28; 64:15). It also warns them that among their children there may be enemies for them (64:14). In order to succeed in this test or trial and be protected against the enmity of their children, it orders the parents to guard themselves and their families through the enabling discipline of the Islamic faith and worship against a Fire whose fuel is human beings and stones (66:6). Among their duties towards their children, it particularly commands the parents to order their families to establish the Prayer, and be diligent in its observance (20:132).

The Qur'an draws the attention to a typical contrast between the states of a believer and unbeliever in respect of their family lives and their respective consequences in the afterlife, as follows:

> Then, as for him who will be given his Record in his right hand, surely he will be reckoned with by an easy reckoning, and will return in joy to his household (prepared for him in Paradise). But as for him who will be given his Record (in his left hand) from behind his back, he will surely pray for destruction, and enter the Flame to roast. For, indeed, he used to be in joyous conceit among his household (in his earthly life). He thought that he would never return (to Allah for judgment). (84:7–14)

> Those (who will be given their Records in their right hands and turn to their households in joy will) say: "We used to be,

when amongst our families, indeed most apprehensive before (most careful and alert for the guidance and eternal life of our family members)." (52:26)

The contrast between the state of a believer and that of an unbeliever is highly significant. An unbeliever condemned to eternal punishment is one who is conceited and joyful among his household in the world. He rejoices in his worldly possessions, of which he is proud, and is indifferent to his Creator and His commands. When he sees the punishment in the Hereafter, he will pray for eternal destruction. However, a believer who is to be rewarded with eternal bliss in the other world is one who is very careful and alert among his family for his own and their guidance and eternal life. So he will rejoice in the Hereafter in the reward he has been given.

Parents should be lenient towards their children. Allah's Messenger, upon him be peace and blessings, said, "Treating those under one's authority well produces prosperity, but an evil nature produces evil fortune."[21] Allah's Messenger, upon him be peace and blessings, was very mild and merciful in his behavior towards his daughter, Fatima, may Allah be pleased with her. 'A'isha, Mother of Believers, says:

> I never saw anyone more like Allah's Messenger, upon him be peace and blessings, in respect of gravity, calm deportment, pleasant disposition, and in respect of talk and speech than Fatima. When she came to visit the Prophet, he got up to welcome her, took her by the hand, kissed her, and made her sit where he was sitting; and when he went to visit her, she got up to welcome him, took him by the hand, kissed him, and made him sit where she was sitting."[22]

At a time when having daughters was despised and some people even buried their daughters alive, Allah's Messenger, upon him be peace and blessings, declared, "If anyone cares for three (or two) daughters, disciplines them, marries them, and does good to them, he will go to Paradise."[23]

4. The duties of siblings towards each other: To love each other, to help each other, and to show each other respect and compassion. There is a very strong bond between brothers and sisters; this must always be maintained. In fact, older siblings deserve great respect, just as parents do. Brothers and sisters who cut their ties with each other over finances or property disagreements cannot be counted as good persons.

Social Relationships[24]

Relations among the members of an Islamic society are based upon two fundamental principles: awareness of the strong Islamic bond of fellowship that links one individual to another, and protecting the individual's rights and the sanctity of his or her life, honor, and property, as guaranteed by Islam. Any words, deeds, or behavior that contravene or threaten these two principles are forbidden, the degree of prohibition depending upon the magnitude of material or moral injury that might result from it.

The Sacredness of Life

Life is extremely valuable in the sight of Islam. For life is the real basis and light of existence. Consciousness, in turn, is the light of life. Life constitutes the foundation of everything and appropriates everything for each living thing. Only through life can a living creature claim that everything belongs to it, that the world is its home and the universe its property conferred by the Owner. See how lonely even a mountain-sized object is without life. Its interactions are restricted to its location, and all that exists in the universe means nothing to it, for it is unconscious of other existents. But since such a minute living being as a honeybee can have close interactions with the universe, particularly with plants and flowers, it can say that the earth is the place where it does business. If life's effect upon this small creature is so great, how much greater will it be upon humanity, as it expands into our consciousness, reason or intellect and heart. Through reason and consciousness (the light of life), we travel through the higher worlds of corporeal and spiritual existence as easily as passing from one room to another. Just as conscious, living beings may visit those worlds in spirit, those worlds come as guests to our mirror-like spirit by being reflected there.

Life is clear evidence of Allah's Unity, the greatest source of His bounty, a most subtle manifestation of His Compassion, and a most hidden and delicate embroidery of His Art. Life is so mysterious and subtle that even the life of plants (the simplest level of life) and the awakening of the life-force in seeds (the beginning of its life) are still not understood fully. Although it is something common to us, it has remained a mystery since the time of Adam, for no person has ever grasped its nature. In its outer (material) and inner (immaterial) aspects, life is pure. Divine Power creates life without the participation of causes, while It uses natural causes to create everything else.

In short, life is the spirit's light, and consciousness is life's light. Since life and consciousness are so important, and a perfect harmony prevails over all creation, the universe displays firm cohesion through life. It is because of this importance of life, it is because Allah's Attributes and Names are manifested through life most brightly and comprehensively that Islam attaches to it extreme importance. And since human life is the most perfect degree of created life standing for the whole of existence, and since whatever is required for the life of all animate beings is also required for the life of a single being, killing a single human being is as monstrous a thing in the sight of the Qur'an as killing the whole of humanity, and saving a single human life is as valuable thing as saving the life of all humanity

> He who kills a soul unless it be (in legal punishment) for murder or for causing disorder and corruption on the earth will be as if he had killed all humankind; and he who saves a life will be as if he had saved the lives of all humankind. (5:32)

The crime is more serious if the killed person was a believer:

> Whoever kills a believer intentionally, his recompense (in the Hereafter) is Hell, therein to abide; and Allah has utterly condemned him, excluded him from His mercy, and prepared for him a tremendous punishment. (4:93)

The Messenger said, "The passing away of the world would mean less to Allah than the murder of a Muslim." and, "Allah may forgive every sin, except for one who dies as an idolater (and an unbeliever) or who kills a believer intentionally."[25] On the basis of these verses and Traditions, Ibn 'Abbas deduced that Allah would not accept any repentance from the murderer.

Ibn 'Umar, may Allah be pleased with him, relates:

> The Prophet, upon him be peace and blessings, said at Mina, "Do you know what day is today?" They (the people) replied, "Allah and His Messenger know better." He said, "Today is the tenth of Dhul-Hijja, the sacred (forbidden) day. Do you know what town is this town?" They replied, "Allah and His Messenger know better." He said, "This is the sacred town (of Mecca)." And do you know what month is this month?" They replied, "Allah and His Messenger know better." He said, "This is the sacred (forbidden) month." He added, "Allah has made your blood, your properties, and your honor sacred to one another like the sanctity of this day of yours in this month of yours, in this town of yours."[26]

The Sanctity of the Lives of Allies and Non-Muslim Residents

Thus far we have quoted texts that warn Muslims against killing or fighting fellow Muslims. But let no one think that the life of a non-Muslim is not safe in a Muslim society, for Allah has declared the life of every person to be sacred, and He guarantees it. This applies as long as non-Muslims do not fight Muslims. If they fight Muslims, the Muslims can fight them in retaliation. However, if the non-Muslims have a treaty with the Muslims or are non-Muslim residents of an Islamic state, their lives are sacred and the Muslims cannot attack them. Moreover, the Qur'an encourages doing good to everyone who is not actively engaged in hostilities towards Muslims:

> Allah does not forbid you, as regards those who do not make war against you on account of your Religion, nor drive you away from your homes, to be kindly to them, and act towards them with equity. Allah surely loves the scrupulously equitable. Allah only forbids you, as regards those who make war against you on account of your Religion and drive you away from your homes, or support others to drive you away, to take them for friends and guardians. Whoever takes them for friends and guardians, those are the wrongdoers. (60:8–9)

Islam even forbids frightening a believer. Allah's Messenger, upon him be and blessings, warns, saying, "It is not lawful for a Muslim that he frightens a Muslim."[27]

Suicide

Whatever applies to murder also applies to suicide. Whoever takes his or her own life, regardless of the method used, has unjustly taken a life that Allah has made sacred. Since people did not create themselves, not even one single cell, their life does not belong to them but is a trust given to them by Allah Almighty. They are not allowed to diminish it, let alone to harm or destroy it. Islam requires Muslims to be resolute in facing hardships. They are not permitted to give up and run away from life's vicissitudes when a tragedy befalls them or some of their hopes are dashed. Indeed, they are created to strive, not to sit idle; for struggle, not for escape. Their faith and character do not permit them to run away from the battlefield of life, and they possess a weapon that never fails and ammunition that is never exhausted: the weapon of unshakable faith and the ammunition of moral steadfastness.

The Sacredness of Honor

Islamic teachings safeguard human dignity and honor and, in fact, regard them as inviolable and sacred. Once while looking at the Ka'ba, 'Abdullah ibn 'Umar, may Allah be pleased with him, remarked, "How great and sacred you are! But the sanctity of a believer is greater than yours." A Muslim's sanctity includes the sanctity of his or her life, honor, and property. The Prophet, upon him be peace and blessings, said, "The gravest sin is going to lengths in talking unjustly against a Muslim's honor, and it is a major sin to abuse twice for abusing once."[28] He also said, "When I was taken up to heaven (during the *Mi'raj*) I passed by people who had nails of copper and were scratching their faces and their breasts. I said, 'Who are these people, Gabriel?' He replied, 'They are those who were given to backbiting and who maligned people's honor.'"[29] He also warned, saying, "If anyone eats once at the cost of a Muslim's honor, Allah will give him a like amount of Hell to eat; if anyone clothes himself with a garment at the cost of a Muslim's honor, Allah will clothe him with a like amount of Hell; and if anyone puts himself in a position of reputation and show, Allah will disgrace him with a place of reputation and show on the Day of Resurrection."[30]

We must also avoid searching for and finding faults with other Muslims. The Messenger warned severely, saying, "O community of people, who believed by their tongue, and belief did not enter their hearts, do not backbite Muslims, and do not search for their faults, for if anyone searches for their faults, Allah will search for his fault, and if Allah searches for the fault of anyone, He disgraces him in his house."[31]

In another Tradition related by Abu Hurayra, may Allah be pleased with him, the Messenger declared, "The servant who conceals the faults of others in this world, Allah will conceal his faults on the Day of Resurrection."[32]

Instead of searching for their faults, we must conceal the faults of a Muslim that are kept hidden. The Messenger, upon him be peace and blessings, says, "He who sees something which should be kept hidden and conceals it will be like one who has brought to life a girl buried alive."[33]

Instead of disgracing Muslims, we must protect their honor in their absence. Allah's Messenger, upon him be peace and blessings, said, "No (Muslim) man will desert a man who is a Muslim in a place where his respect may be violated and his honor aspersed without Allah deserting him in a place where he wishes for His help; and no (Muslim) man will help a Muslim in a place where his honor may be maligned and his respect violated without Allah helping him in a place where he wishes for His help."[34]

The Prophet, upon him be peace and blessings, also said, "The believer is the believer's mirror, and the believer is the believer's brother who guards him against loss and protects him in his absence."[35]

We must mention other Muslims, including the dead, with their virtues. The Messenger, upon him be peace and blessings, orders, "Make mention of the virtues of your dead, and refrain from (mentioning) their evils."[36]

Loving and Supporting Each Other and Sharing Each Other's Pains and Troubles

Muslims must love each other for Allah's sake and inform each other of this. Anas ibn Malik, may Allah be pleased with him, narrates:

A man was with the Prophet, upon him be peace and blessings, and a man passed by him and said, "Messenger of Allah! I love this man." Allah's Messenger, upon him be peace and blessings, then asked, "Have you informed him?" He replied, "No." He said, "Inform him." He then went to him and said, "I love you for Allah's sake." He replied, "May He for Whose sake you love me love you!"[37]

The Prophet, upon him be peace and blessings, said, "None will have the sweetness (delight) of faith until he loves a person and loves him only for Allah's sake, and until it becomes dearer to him to be thrown in the fire than to revert to unbelief after Allah has brought him out of it, and until Allah and His Messenger become dearer to him than anything else."[38]

When Muslims meet, they greet each other and shake hands. The Prophet, upon him be peace and blessings, said, "If two Muslims meet, shake hands, praise Allah, and ask Him for forgiveness, they will be forgiven."[39] He also said, "Two Muslims will not meet and shake hands without having their sins forgiven them before they separate."[40] When the Messenger, upon him be peace and blessings, met his Companions especially after the Friday congregational Prayers and '*Iyd* Prayers, he shook hands with them.[41] Muslim scholars unanimously agree that shaking hands (*musafaha*) is a *sunna* act, a practice of the Prophet worthy of being emulated.

Muslims help and support each other and share each other's pains and troubles. Allah's Messenger, upon him be peace and blessings, said, "You see the believers as regards their being merciful among themselves and showing love among themselves and being kind, resembling one body, so that if any part of the body is not well then the whole body shares the sleeplessness (insomnia) and fever with it."[42] In another narration, he said, "A believer to another believer is like a building whose different parts reinforce each other."[43]

In another, comprehensive Tradition, Allah's Messenger, upon him be peace and blessings, describes how the relationships between Muslims must be, as follows:

> A Muslim is the brother (sister) of a Muslim. He neither oppresses him nor humiliates him nor looks down upon him. The piety is here (and while saying so he pointed towards his chest thrice). It is a serious evil for a Muslim that he should look down upon his brother Muslim. All things of a Muslim are inviolable for his brother in faith: his blood, his wealth and his honor.[44]

Allah's Messenger orders that a Muslim must help his brother or sister whether he or she is the oppressor or oppressed, saying, "A

person should help his brother whether he is an oppressor or an oppressed. If he is the oppressor he should prevent him from doing it,
for that is his help; and if he is the oppressed he should be helped
(against oppression).[45]

More than mutual helping among the Muslims, the Qur'an exhorts Muslims to prefer their brothers and sisters over their own
selves, and praises the *Ansar* (the Helpers—the Muslims of Medina
during the Prophet's time) for their altruism. It says:

> Those who, before their coming, had their abode (in Medina),
> preparing it as a home for Islam and faith, love those who
> emigrate to them for Allah's sake, and in their hearts do not
> begrudge what they have been given; and (indeed) they prefer
> them over themselves, even though poverty be their own lot.
> And all those who come after them (and follow in their foot-
> steps) pray, "O our Lord! Forgive us and our brothers (and
> sisters) in Religion who have preceded us in faith, and let not
> our hearts entertain any ill-feeling against any of the believers.
> O our Lord! You are All-Forgiving, All-Compassionate (espe-
> cially toward Your believing servants). (59:9–10)

Regarding mutual helping, the Qur'an reminds us of an important point. It orders:

> Help one another in virtue and goodness, and righteousness
> and piety, and do not help one another in sinful, iniquitous
> acts and hostility; (in all your actions) keep from disobedience
> to Allah in reverence for Him and piety. Surely Allah is severe
> in retribution. (5:2)

Meeting a Muslim brother or sister with a cheerful countenance
is charity. Allah's Messenger, upon him be peace and blessings, declared, "Don't consider anything insignificant out of good things even
if it is that you meet your brother with a cheerful countenance."[46]

The Sanctity of Property

Muslims are permitted to earn as much as they desire, as long as
they do so through lawful means and increase their wealth through

lawful investments, and they do not indulge in luxury and debauchery. However, Islam warns against attachment to wealth and the world and leading a luxurious, dissipated life, and exhorts believers to spend in Allah's way for the needy and Allah's cause. Since Islam sanctions the right to personal property, it protects it through moral exhortation and legislation from robbery, theft, and fraud. The Messenger mentioned its sanctity in the same sentence with the sanctity of life and honor, and considered stealing contradictory to faith: "A thief is not a believer while he (she) is engaged in stealing,"[47] and, "It is *haram* for a Muslim to take (so much as) a stick without its owner's consent."

Islam also orders returning something borrowed. Allah's Messenger, upon him be peace and blessings, said, "None of you should take the property of his brother in amusement (i.e. jest), nor in earnest. If anyone takes the staff of his brother, he should return it."[48]

Privacy of Family Life

According to Islam, the privacy of family life is essential. The Qur'an orders us to obtain the permission of its residents before we enter any private dwelling and to greet them with peace:

> O you who believe! Do not enter dwellings other than your own until you have ascertained the permission of their residents and have greeted them with peace. Your doing so is what is good and appropriate for you, so that you may be mindful (of good manners and proper courtesy). Then, if you find no one in them, do not enter them until you have permission to enter. If you are asked to go back, then go back (without feeling offended). It is a purer way for you. Allah has full knowledge of all that you do. (24:27–28)

Huzayl, may Allah be pleased with him, narrates:

> A man came. He stood facing the door. The Prophet, upon him be peace and blessings, warned him, saying, "Away from it, (stand) this side or that side. Asking permission is meant to escape from the look of an eye."[49]

It is forbidden to peep into the house of anybody. The Prophet, upon him be peace and blessings, said, "If anyone peeps into the house of people without their permission and he knocks out his eye, no responsibility is incurred for his eye."[50]

The only entrance to a house is its door, so the Qur'an orders us to enter dwellings through their doors:

> It is not virtue that you enter dwellings from the backs of them, but virtue is (the state of) one who strives to attain righteousness and piety. So come to dwellings (in the normal way) by their doors; and strive to obey Allah in due reverence for Him and piety so that you may prosper. (2:189)

The privacy of family life is something which should be preserved not only from others but also among the members of the family. For example, the Qur'an orders parents to teach their children to ask for their permission to enter upon them at the times of privacy during the day:

> O you who believe! Let those whom your right hands possess (as slaves), as well as those of you (your children) who have not yet reached puberty, ask for your permission (before they come into your private room) at three times (of the day)—before the Morning Prayer, and when you lay aside your garments in the middle of the day for rest, and after the Night Prayer. These are your three times of privacy. Beyond these occasions, there is no blame on you nor on them if they come in without permission—they are bound to move about you, some of you attending on others. Thus, Allah makes clear for you (the instructions in) the Revelations. Allah is All-Knowing, All-Wise. And when your children reach puberty, let them ask you for permission (whenever they want to enter your private room), even as those (who have already reached the same age) before them ask for it. Thus, Allah makes clear for you (the instructions in) His Revelations. Allah is All-Knowing, All-Wise. (24:58–59)

Guarding the secrets or privacy of family life is a duty upon the members of the family. The Qur'an praises especially women who guard the privacy of their family life (4:34).

Individual Responsibility and the Restrictedness of Human Freedom

A human is not some kind of being that has absolute freedom and is able to do or attain whatever he or she wishes. It is Allah Who has created the universe and humankind. No one has any choice about whether they come to the world or not; when and where they are born; in what family they will come to the world; when they will depart from the world; nor in the determination of their color, race, physical body, or sex. So, it is also Allah Who has established the conditions of life in the world and the law of causality (what happens to humans as a result of their actions); and it is also He Who has established what deed will bring reward or punishment in the Hereafter. In sum, human beings have not been given either absolute freedom or absolute autonomy. It is true that they have a free will but it is restricted. So, humans are able to do some things within the scope of their free will and are responsible for their choices and acts. The Qur'an declares:

> Or will human attain whatever he craves? But (whatever human desires, be it to serve his higher good, or to serve his carnal appetites) to Allah belong the after(life) and the former (life). (53:24–25)

Every human being is responsible for their acts to the extent of their affects. No one can and is made to bear the burden of another:

> That no soul, as bearer of burden, is made to bear the burden of another. And that human has only that for which he labors, and his labor will be brought forth to be seen. And afterward he will be repaid for it with fullest payment. And in your Lord, everything ends. (53:38–42)

Preserving the Unity and Agreement among Muslims and Making Peace among Them

Unity, agreement, accord and social solidarity are very important in a Muslim community. The Qur'an orders:

> And obey Allah and His Messenger, and do not dispute with one another, or else you may lose heart and your power and energy desert you; and remain steadfast. Surely, Allah is with those who remain steadfast. (8:46)

The Qur'an also orders:

> And hold fast all together to the rope of Allah, and never be divided. Remember Allah's favor upon you: you were once enemies, and He reconciled your hearts so that through His favor, you became like brothers. You stood on the brink of a pit of fire, and He delivered you from it. Thus, Allah makes His signs of truth clear to you that you may be guided (to the Straight Path in all matters, and be steadfast on it). (3:103)

The Qur'an warns Muslims against internal divisions, and threatens those who follow a way other than that of the believers, saying:

> Be not as those who split into parties and followed different ways after the manifest truths had come to them. Those are the ones for whom is a tremendous punishment. (3:105)

> While whoever cuts himself off from the Messenger after the guidance (to what is truest and best in thought, belief, and conduct) has become clear to him, and follows a way other than that of the believers (for whom it is impossible to agree unanimously on a way that leads to error), We leave him (to himself) on the way he has turned to, and land him in Hell to roast there: how evil a destination to arrive at! (4:115)

In order for the Muslims to be able to hold fast altogether to the rope of Allah and thus to preserve the unity among them and be saved from internal divisions, the Qur'an orders:

> There must be among you a community calling to good, and enjoining and actively promoting what is right, and forbidding and trying to prevent evil (in appropriate ways). They are those who are the prosperous. (3:104)

What follows is another important command of the Qur'an so that Muslims can preserve the unity among them and the order and security on the earth:

> Those who disbelieve—they are friends and protectors of one another (especially against you). Unless you do it also (i.e. maintain solidarity among the believers), there will be unrest on the earth and great corruption. (8:73)

Making peace among the disagreeing Muslims without any delay is another significant order of the Qur'an:

> The believers are but brothers, so make peace between your brothers; and keep from disobedience to Allah in reverence for Him and piety (particularly in your duties toward one another as brothers), so that you may be shown mercy (granted a good, virtuous life in the world as individuals and as a community, and eternal happiness in the Hereafter). (49:10)

Making peace among the Muslims is so vital that all the Muslims may have to fight against a rebellious party among them until they comply with Allah's decree. The Qur'an says:

> If two parties of believers fall to fighting, make peace between them (and act promptly). But if one of them aggressively encroaches on the rights of the other, then fight you all against the aggressive side until they comply with Allah's decree (concerning the matter). If they comply, then make peace between them with justice and be scrupulously equitable. Surely Allah loves the scrupulously equitable. (49:9)

Muslims must refrain from spreading any cause or rumor of disagreement among themselves or in their community. Any disagreement among them must be referred to those invested with authority and be solved according to Allah's Book and the Prophet's

Sunna. Reconciliation and peace among them may require the appointment of arbiters. The Qur'an says:

> Whenever any news comes to them, related to (public) security or alarm, they go about spreading it (without ascertaining if the news is true or not, and without thinking about whether it is beneficial or harmful to spread it). Whereas if they would but refer it to the Messenger and to those among them (in the community) who are entrusted with authority, those from among them who are competent to investigate it would bring to light what it is really about. (O believers!) Save for Allah's grace and mercy upon you (in illuminating your way and guiding you with Revelation and His Messenger, and protecting you against your enemies and wrong ways), all but a few (of you) would have been (deceived by the hypocrites and) following Satan. (4:83)

> O you who believe! Obey Allah and obey the Messenger, and those from among you who are invested with authority; and if you are to dispute among yourselves about anything, refer it to Allah and the Messenger, if indeed you believe in Allah and the Last Day. This is the best (for you), and fairest in the end. (4:59)

> And if you fear that a breach might occur between a couple, appoint an arbiter from among his people and an arbiter from among her people. If they both want to set things aright, Allah will bring about reconciliation between them. Assuredly, Allah is All-Knowing, All-Aware. (4:35)

Any discomfort or objection in the face of Islam's verdict or judgment is a sign of lack of sound belief and submission to Allah and His Messenger. The Qur'an warns:

> But no! By your Lord, they do not (truly) believe unless they make you the judge regarding any dispute between them, and then find not the least vexation within themselves over what you have decided, and surrender in full submission. (4:65)

Sila ar-Rahm

Rahm means the mother's womb, therefore *sila ar-rahm* is a religious term used to describe the continued relationships between relatives and the duties required by these relationships. They mainly consist of visiting one's parents, brothers and sisters, and relatives, asking after them, helping and supporting them, and treating them kindly and generously. Islam attaches great importance to relations with people, most especially between close relatives, beginning with mother and father. The Prophet said, "The word *ar-Rahm* (womb) derives its name from '*Ar-Rahman*' (i.e. the All-Merciful). So whosoever keeps good relations with it (the womb, i.e., kith and kin), Allah will keep good relations with him, and whosoever will sever it, Allah too will sever His relations with him."[51]

The Qur'an declares:

> O humankind! In due reverence for your Lord, keep from disobedience to Him Who created you from a single human self, and from it created its mate, and from the pair of them, scattered abroad a multitude of men and women. In due reverence for Allah, keep from disobedience to Him in Whose name you make demands of one another, and (duly observe) the rights of the wombs (i.e. of kinship, thus observing piety in your relations with Allah and with human beings). Allah is ever watchful over you. (4:1)

While praising some believers, the Qur'an presents them as having the following virtues:

> And those who unite the bonds Allah has commanded to be joined (among kin as a requirement of blood relationship, and among people as required by human social interdependence), and stand in awe of their Lord, and fearful of (facing) the most evil reckoning.... (13:21)

Khalid ibn Zayd (Abu Ayyub al-Ansari), may Allah be pleased with him, relates a narration in which a man came and asked the Prophet, "O Messenger of Allah, can you tell me an act of worship by which I may enter Paradise?" The Messenger, upon him be peace and blessings, replied as follows:

> Worship Allah, do not associate any partners with Him, do the daily Prayers, pay the *Zakah*, and visit your parents.[52]

The Prophet also said, "The person who severs the bond of kinship will not enter Paradise."[53]

It is Haram to Sever Ties with a Fellow Muslim

It is *haram* for Muslims to shun, break ties, or turn away from a fellow Muslim. If two Muslims quarrel with each other, they may be allowed a cooling-off period of three days at the most, after which they must seek reconciliation and peace, overcoming their pride, anger, and hatred.[54] The Messenger, upon him peace and blessings, also warned, "There is no sin more fitted to have punishment meted out by Allah to its perpetrator in advance in this world along with what He stores up for him in the next world than oppression and severing ties of relationship."[55]

Settling Disputes

While it is incumbent upon disputants to settle their differences in an Islamic fashion, the Muslim community also has a responsibility in this regard. As it is based upon mutual caring and cooperation, the Muslim community cannot stand by passively and watch its members dispute and quarrel with each other, and thereby permit the conflict to grow larger. Those who command respect and authority in the community are obliged to come forward to set things right with absolute impartiality and without allowing themselves to become emotionally involved with either side. The Qur'an orders:

> If two parties of believers fall to fighting, make peace between them (and act promptly). But if one of them aggressively encroaches on the rights of the other, then fight you all against the aggressive side until they comply with Allah's decree (con-

cerning the matter). If they comply, then make peace between them with justice and be scrupulously equitable. Surely Allah loves the scrupulously equitable. The believers are but brothers, so make peace between your brothers; and keep from disobedience to Allah in reverence for Him and piety (particularly in your duties toward one another as brothers), so that you may be shown mercy (granted a good, virtuous life in the world as individuals and as a community, and eternal happiness in the Hereafter). (49:9–10)

The Prophet, upon him be peace and blessings, said, "Shall I not inform you of something more excellent in degree than (voluntary) fasting, Prayer and almsgiving (*sadaqah*)?" The people replied, "Yes, Prophet of Allah!" He said, "It is putting things right between people."[56]

The Qur'an also orders magnanimity and prayer in the relations of Muslims with each other:

Those who, before their coming, had their abode (in Medina), preparing it as a home for Islam and faith, love those who emigrate to them for Allah's sake, and in their hearts do not begrudge what they have been given; and (indeed) they prefer them over themselves, even though poverty be their own lot. And all those who come after them (and follow in their footsteps) pray: "O our Lord! Forgive us and our brothers (and sisters) in Religion who have preceded us in faith, and let not our hearts entertain any ill-feeling against any of the believers. O our Lord! You are All-Forgiving, All-Compassionate (especially towards Your believing servants)." (59:9–10)

"Let not some people deride other people"

In 49:10-12, Allah proscribes several things related to preserving Muslim brotherhood and sisterhood and states what this implies with regard to that which people consider sacred. The first of these is the prohibition of mocking, deriding, and scoffing at others:

O you who believe! Let not some people among you deride another people; it may be that the latter are better than the former. Nor let some women deride other women; it may be that the latter are better than the former. (48:11)

"Do not slander"

The second prohibition is against *lamz*, which literally means "piercing and stabbing." Here it is used to mean finding fault, as the person who finds fault with others is doing something similar to piercing them with a sword or stabbing them with a dagger—and perhaps the wound inflicted by the tongue is more lasting. The form of prohibition expressed in 49:11 (*Nor defame one another [and provoke the same for yourselves in retaliation]*) is very subtle, for it means not to slander each other. This meaning is derived from the Qur'an's viewing the Muslim community as one body in its mutual concerns and responsibilities, so that whoever slanders a fellow Muslim in effect slanders himself or herself.

Slandering especially innocent women is one of the most heinous crimes deserving a great punishment. The Qur'an orders:

> Those who accuse chaste, honorable women (of illicit sexual relations) but do not produce four male witnesses (who will witness that they personally saw the act being committed): flog them with eighty stripes, and do not accept from them any testimony ever after. They are indeed transgressors. (24:4)

> Those who falsely accuse chaste women, who are unaware of devious ways of corruption and are believers, are cursed in the world and the Hereafter, and for them is a mighty punishment. (24:23)

Committing a crime or a sin and then throwing the blame on an innocent person is a monstrous act decisively forbidden by the Qur'an:

> And he who earns a wrong or sin, and then throws the blame on an innocent person, has thereby laid upon himself (the additional burden of) a calumny and a flagrant sin. (4:112)

We must refrain from accusing other Muslims and judging them. The Prophet, upon him be peace and blessings, warned, saying, "If somebody accuses another of *fisq* (sinfulness, wickedness) or accuses him of unbelief, such an accusation will revert to him (i.e. the accuser) if the accused one is innocent."[57]

Islam also forbids mocking and vilifying people. The Qur'an reads:

> There was among My servants a party who would pray, "Our Lord! We have believed, so forgive us, and have mercy on us, for You are the Best of the merciful." You used to take them in mockery, so much so that your hostilities to them caused you to forget My remembrance, and you simply persisted in laughing at them. But look, today I have rewarded them for what they endured patiently, so that they are those who are the triumphant. (23:109–111)

> Woe to every one who slanders and vilifies—who (sees himself above others because he) has amassed wealth and (without expending it in Allah's cause and for the needy) counts it (in greedy love for it). He thinks that his wealth will make him last forever! (104:1–3)

Avoiding Bad Nicknames

The Qur'an also forbids giving one a bad name and insulting others with nicknames that they dislike:

> Nor insult one another with nicknames (that your brothers and sisters dislike). Evil is using names with vile meaning after (those so addressed have accepted) the faith (doing so is like replacing a mark of faith with a mark of transgression). Whoever (does that and then) does not turn to Allah in repentance (giving up doing so), those are indeed wrongdoers. (49:11)

Calling People by Good Names or the Best of the Titles They Like

Islam not only forbids giving a person a bad name and insulting others with nicknames that they dislike but also orders calling people by good names.

The Prophet, upon him be peace and blessings, said, "On the Day of Resurrection you will be called by your names and by your father's names, so give yourselves good names."[58] He would say that such names as 'Abdullah, 'Abdur-Rahman, and Ibrahim were most lovable in Allah's sight, and advise people to call their children by them.[59] The Prophet, upon him be peace and blessings, would also change names with bad meanings.[60]

Avoiding Suspicion

Islam seeks to establish its society on a clean conscience and mutual trust, not on doubt, suspicion, accusation, and mistrust. Hence it mentions the fourth prohibition designed to safeguard what people hold sacred: *O you who believe! Avoid much suspicion, for some suspicion is a grave sin (liable to Allah's punishment)* (49:12). Sinful suspicion is defined as ascribing evil motives to others. Muslims cannot impute such motives to fellow Muslims without justification and clear evidence. Given that the basic assumption is that people are innocent, mere suspicion should not be allowed to cause an innocent person to be accused. The Qur'an severely warns against affronting Muslims without their having done any wrong to deserve it: *Those who affront believing men and believing women without their having done any wrong to deserve it, they have surely burdened themselves with calumny and a blatant sin* (33:58).

As suspicion or thinking ill of a Muslim is a sin, acting in a way which will lead others to harbor suspicion about one is also a sin. Safiyya bint Huyay, Mother of Believers, may Allah be pleased with her, narrates that she went to Allah's Messenger, upon him be peace and blessings, while he was in *i'tikaf* (staying in the mosque) during the last ten nights of the month of Ramadan. She spoke to him for a while at night and then she got up to return home. The Prophet, upon him be peace and blessings, got up to accompany her, and when they reached the gate of the mosque opposite the dwelling place of Umm Salama, Mother of Believers, may Allah be pleased with her, two Ansari men passed by, and greeting Allah's Messenger, upon him be peace and blessings, they quickly went ahead. Allah's Messenger, upon him be peace and blessings, said to them, "Do not be in a hurry. This is Safiyya, the daughter of Huyay." They said, "All glory be to Allah! O Allah's Messenger (how dare we suspect you)!" That was a great thing for both of them. The Prophet, upon him be peace and blessings, then said, "Satan runs in the body of Adam's son (i.e. man) as his blood circulates in his blood vessels, and I was afraid that he (Satan) might insert an evil thought in your hearts."[61]

Although we are commanded to have a good opinion of all Muslims, we should avoid exaggerated praise. We cannot know exactly anybody's position in Allah's sight. A man was mentioned in the presence of the Prophet, upon him be peace and blessings, and another man praised him greatly. The Prophet, upon him be peace and blessings, said, "May Allah's mercy be on you! You have cut the neck of your friend." The Prophet repeated this sentence many times and said, "If someone feels he cannot do but praise a friend of his, he should say, 'I think that he is such a good man,' if he really thinks that he is such. Allah is the One Who will call him to account (for his deeds as He knows his reality), and no one can sanctify anybody before Allah."[62]

Spying

Mistrust of others produces evil thoughts in the mind, while outwardly it leads a person towards spying. But since Islam establishes its society upon inner and outer purity, just as spying follows suspicion, the prohibition of spying comes immediately after that of suspicion (49:12). Prying into other peoples' private affairs and spying on their secrets is not permitted, even if they are engaged in sin, as long as they do it privately. Allah's Messenger, upon him be peace and blessings, said:

> Avoid suspicion, for suspicion is the gravest lie in talk; and do not be inquisitive about one another, and do not spy upon one another, and do not feel envy of the other, and nurse no malice, and nurse no aversion and hostility against one another. And be fellow brothers (sisters) and servants of Allah.[63]

Backbiting

The sixth evil forbidden in the verses cited above is backbiting (*ghiyba*): *And do not ... backbite one another. Would any of you love to eat the flesh of his dead brother? You would abhor it!* (49:12). The verse likens backbiting to the eating of one's dead brother's (or sister's) flesh. The Messenger, upon him be peace and blessings, wanted to drive home the meaning of backbiting to his Companions through questions and answers. He asked them, "Do you know what backbiting is?" They replied, "Allah and His Messenger know best." He said, "It is saying something about your brother (sister) which he (she) would dislike." Someone asked, "What if I say something about my brother (sister) that is true?" The Messenger replied, "If what you say of him (her) is true, it is backbiting; if it is not true, you have slandered him (her)."[64]

'A'isha, Mother of Believers, may Allah be pleased with her, narrated:

> I said to the Prophet, upon him be peace and blessings, "It is enough for you in Safiyya that she is such-and-such (meaning that she was short-statured)." The Prophet replied, "You have said a word which would change the sea if it were mixed in it."[65]

What follows is what Said Nursi writes about backbiting based on the verse prohibiting it:

> This statement (*Would any of you love to eat the flesh of his dead brother?*) reprimands the backbiter with six degrees of repri-

mand and restrains him or her from this sin with six degrees of severity:

- The *hamzah*, marking the interrogative (and here translated as *would*) at the beginning of the sentence reaches into all the words of the verse, so that each of them carries an interrogative accent.
- Thus, at the very beginning the *hamzah* in itself asks, "Do you have no intelligence with which you ask and answer, so that you fail to perceive how abominable this thing is?"
- The second word, *love*, asks through *hamzah*, "Is it that your heart, with which you love or hate, is so spoiled that you love a most repugnant thing like backbiting?"
- Third, the phrase, *any of you*, asks, "What has happened to your sense of the nature and responsibility of society and civilization that you dare to accept something so poisonous to social life?"
- Fourth, the phrase, *to eat the flesh*, asks, "What has happened to your sense of humanity that you are tearing your friend to pieces with your teeth like a wild animal?"
- Fifth, the phrase, *of his brother*, asks, "Do you have no human tenderness, no sense of kinship, that you sink your teeth into some innocent person to whom you are tied by numerous links of brotherhood? Do you have no intelligence that you bite into your own limbs with your teeth, in such a senseless fashion?"
- Sixth, the word, *dead*, asks, "Where is your conscience? Is your nature so corrupt that you commit such a disgusting act as eating the flesh of your dead brother who deserves much respect?"

According, then, to the total meaning of the verse and the indications of each of these words, slander and backbiting are repugnant to the intelligence, and to the heart, to humanity and conscience, to human nature, the Religion, and social fellowship. You see, then, that the verse condemns backbiting in six degrees in a very concise and exact manner and restrains people from it in six miraculous ways.

Backbiting is a shameful weapon and most commonly used by people of enmity, envy, and obstinacy; no self-respecting, honorable human being would ever demean themselves by resorting to such a vile weapon.

Backbiting consists of speaking about an absent person in a way that would repel or annoy him or her if he or she were present and were to hear. If the words uttered are true, that is backbiting; if they are not, this is both backbiting and slander and, therefore, is a doubly loathsome sin.

Backbiting can be permissible in a very few, particular circumstances:

- A person who has been wronged can present a formal complaint to some officer, so that with their help, a wrong may be righted and justice restored.

- If a person contemplating co-operation or marriage with another comes to hold counsel with you, and you say to them, disinterestedly and purely for the sake of their benefit, and in order to counsel them properly, without any further motive, "Do not do that business with that person; it will be to your disadvantage."

- If a person says only by way of factual description, not to expose to disgrace or notoriety, "That crippled one went to such and such a place."

- If the person being criticized is an open and unashamed sinner; that is, far from being ashamed of it, they take pride in the sins they commit— if they take pleasure in their wrongdoing and commit sins openly.

In these particular cases, backbiting may be permissible, provided it is done disinterestedly and purely for the sake of truth and in the collective interest. Otherwise, backbiting is like a fire that consumes good deeds in the manner of a flame eating up wood.

If one has engaged in backbiting or listened to it willingly, one should seek Allah's forgiveness, saying, "O Allah, forgive me and the one whom I backbit," and when he meets the person about whom they spoke ill, they should say to them, "Forgive me!"[66]

Spreading Gossip

Another evil, which usually accompanies backbiting and is strictly forbidden by Islam, is gossiping. This is defined as passing on to others what you hear from someone in such a way that will cause dissension among people, sour their relationships, or increase already existing bitterness between them.

Allah's Messenger, upon him be peace and blessings, never liked that someone would come to him and say bad things about others. He said, "None of my Companions must tell me anything about anyone, for I like to come out to you with no ill-feelings."[67] 'Abdullah ibn 'Abbas, may Allah be pleased with him, relates:

> Allah's Messenger, upon him be peace and blessings, passed by two graves and said, "Both of them (persons in the grave) are being tortured, and they are not being tortured for a major sin. This one used not to save himself from being soiled with his urine, and the other used to go about with calumnies (among the people, e.g., one goes to a person and tells him that so and so says about him such and such evil things)." The Prophet, upon him be peace and blessings, then asked for a green leaf of a date-palm tree, split it into two pieces and planted one on each grave and said, "It is hoped that their punishment may be abated till those two pieces of the leaf get dried."[68]

Racial and Color Discrimination

There is no special distinction for people with a certain skin color or who belong to a particular "race" of humanity. Muslims cannot be a partisan of one race against another, and of one people against another. Material or biological origin cannot be a source of superiority. What caused Satan to rebel against Allah's order to prostrate before Adam in the sense of admitting his superiority was his claim of superiority to a human due to his origin:

> (Allah) said: "O *Iblis*! What is the matter with you that you are not among those who have prostrated?" (*Iblis*) said: "I am not one to prostrate myself before a mortal, whom You have created from dried, sounding clay, from molded dark mud." (Allah) said: "Then get you down out of it; surely You are one rejected (from My mercy). "And cursing is upon you until the Day of Judgment." (15:32–35)

The Qur'an describes tribalism or racism as zealotry particular to the Age of Ignorance, and declares that it is only Allah's consciousness, piety, and righteousness which is the sole source of superiority:

> When those who disbelieved harbored in their hearts fierce zealotry (coming from egotism, tribalism, and feuding), the zealotry particular to the Age of Ignorance, Allah sent down His (gift of) inner peace and reassurance on His Messenger and on the believers, and bound them to the Word of faith, piety, and reverence for Allah. They were most worthy of it and entitled to it. And Allah has full knowledge of everything. (48:26)

> O humankind! Surely We have created you from a single (pair of) male and female, and made you into tribes and families so that you may know one another (and so build mutuality and co-operative relationships, not so that you may take pride in your differences of race or social rank, or breed enmities). Surely the noblest, most honorable of you in Allah's sight is the one best in piety, righteousness, and reverence for Allah. Surely Allah is All-Knowing, All-Aware. (49:13)

Racism is one of the severest problems of our age. When Allah's Messenger, upon him be peace and blessings, was raised as a Prophet, the attitudes behind racism were prevalent in Mecca in the guise of tribalism. The Quraysh considered themselves (in particular) and Arabs (in general) as being superior to all other people. Allah's Messenger, upon him be peace and blessings, came with this Divine message and proclaimed it, explaining, "No Arab is superior to a non-Arab, and no white person is superior to a black person."[69]; and, "If a black Abyssinian Muslim is to rule over Muslims, he should be obeyed."[70]

Allah's Messenger, upon him be peace and blessings, eradicated color-based racism and discrimination so successfully that, for example, 'Umar once said of Bilal, who was black, "Bilal is our master, and was emancipated by our master Abu Bakr."[71] Once Abu Dharr got so angry with Bilal that he insulted him: "You son of a black woman!" Bilal came to Allah's Messenger, upon him be peace and blessings, and reported the incident in tears. The Messenger, upon him be peace and blessings, reproached Abu Dharr, "Do you still have a sign of Jahiliyyah (the Time of Ignorance)?" Full of repentance, Abu Dharr lay on the ground and said, "I won't raise my head (meaning he would not get up) unless Bilal puts his foot on it to pass over it." Bilal forgave him, and they were reconciled.[72] Zayd ibn Harithah, a slave emancipated by Allah's Messenger, upon him be peace and blessings, was his adopted son before the Revelation banned adoption as a legal procedure. The Prophet, upon him be peace and blessings, married him to Zaynab bint Jahsh, one of the noblest (and non-black) among the Arab Muslim women. In addition, he chose Zayd as the commander of the Muslim army that was sent against the Byzantine Empire, even though it included such leading Companions as Abu Bakr, 'Umar, Ja'far ibn Abi Talib (the cousin of Allah's Messenger, upon him be peace and blessings), and Khalid ibn Walid (even then famed for his genius as a military commander).[73] Further, the Prophet, upon him be peace and blessings, appointed Zayd's son Usama to command the army he formed just before his death. Included therein were such leading Companions as Abu Bakr, 'Umar, Khalid, Abu 'Ubaydah, Talha, and Zubayr, may Allah be pleased with them. This established in the Muslims' hearts and minds that superiority is not by birth or color or blood, but by righteousness and devotion to Allah.

During his caliphate, 'Umar paid Usama a higher salary than his own son, 'Abdullah. When his son asked why, 'Umar replied, "My son, I do so because I know Allah's Messenger, upon him be peace and blessings, loved Usama's father more than your father, and Usama more than you."[74]

We should note that the prohibition of racism does not mean that we should not love our tribe or nation. Allah's Messenger, upon him be peace and blessings, even encouraged us to defend our tribe or nation as long as it should not be in wrongdoing or sin.[75] What he forbade is defending or helping our tribe or nation in wrongdoing. Wathila ibn al-Asqa' asked him, "Messenger of Allah! What is party spirit (or disapproved partisanship)?" He replied, "That you should help your people in wrongdoing."[76]

Equality in Enjoying the Basic Human Rights and Freedoms

Differences of race, color, family, social status, and wealth cannot be a cause of superiority among people. Allah's Messenger declares that all people are as equal as the teeth of a comb (in being human).[77] Therefore, everyone is also equal before the law. 'A'isha, Mother of Believers, reported that the Quraysh had been anxious about a Makhzumi woman who had committed theft, and said, "Who will speak to Allah's Messenger, upon him be peace and blessings, about her (to intercede on her behalf)? They said, "Who dares but Usama, the loved one of Allah's Messenger?" So Usama spoke to him. Thereupon Allah's Messenger, upon him be peace and blessings, said, "Do you intercede regarding one of the punishments prescribed by Allah?" He then stood up and addressed (people) saying, "O people! Those who have lived before you were destroyed, because (as a primary reason for their destruction) if anyone of high rank committed theft amongst them, they spared him; but if anyone of low rank committed theft, they inflicted the prescribed punishment upon him. By Allah, if Fatima, daughter of Muhammad, were to steal, I would have her hand cut off."[78]

Equality in enjoying basic human rights and freedoms is the source of lawful retribution or the inviolate values demanding retaliation:

> A sacred month is retributive for another sacred month, and the inviolate values demand retaliation. So whoever attacks you, attack them in like manner as they attacked you. Nevertheless, fear Allah and remain within the bounds of piety and righteousness, and know that Allah is with the God-revering, pious. (2:194)

However, this does not mean that Islam does not encourage tolerance and forgiveness. Rather, although it has recognized retribution as a principle of law because of the equality of people and equality in enjoying the basic human rights and freedoms, it earnestly encourages reconciliation, tolerance, and forgiveness in mutual relations:

> The recompense of an evil deed can only be an evil equal to it; but whoever pardons and makes reconciliation, his reward is due from Allah. Surely He does not love the wrongdoers. But whoever defends himself and restores his right (in the lawful way) after he has been wronged—against such there is no route (of blame and retaliation). The route (of blame and retaliation) is only against those who wrong people and behave rebelliously on earth, offending against all right. For such there is a painful punishment. But, indeed, whoever shows patience and forgives (the wrong done to him), surely that is among meritorious things requiring great resolution to fulfill. (42:40–43)

Human Rights in Islam

Islam gave humanity an ideal code of human rights fourteen centuries ago. These rights seek to confer honor and dignity on humanity and to eliminate exploitation, oppression, and injustice.

These human rights are rooted firmly in the belief that Allah, and Allah alone, is the Source of all human rights. Due to their Divine origin, no ruler, government, assembly, or authority can curtail or violate in any way the human rights conferred by Allah, nor can they be surrendered if they are to remain Muslims.

Human rights are an integral part of the overall Islamic order, and all Muslim governments and organs of society must implement them in letter and in spirit within that order's framework. These rights, as compiled by eminent Muslim scholars based on the Qur'an and the Sunna, can be enumerated as follows:

- All people are equal, and no one shall enjoy a privilege or suffer a disadvantage or discrimination due to his or her race, color, sex, origin, or language.

- All people are born free.
- Slavery and forced labor are abhorrent.
- Conditions shall be established to preserve, protect, and honor the institution of family as the basis of all social life.
- Both the rulers and the ruled are subject to, and equal before, the law.
- Only those commands that conform to the law must be obeyed.
- All worldly power is considered a sacred trust to be exercised within the limits prescribed by the law, in a manner approved by it, and with due regard for its priorities.
- All economic resources shall be treated as Divine blessings bestowed upon humanity and shall be enjoyed by all, in accordance with the rules and values set out in the Qur'an and the Sunna.
- All public affairs shall be determined and conducted by mutual consultation, and the authority to administer them shall be exercised according to this consensus.
- Everyone shall undertake obligations proportionate to their capacity and shall be held responsible pro rata for their deeds.
- If a person's rights are infringed upon, he or she shall be assured of appropriate remedial measures in accordance with the law.
- No one shall be deprived of his or her rights guaranteed by the law, except by its authority and to the extent permitted by it.
- Every individual shall have the right to bring legal action against anyone who commits a crime against society as a whole or against any of its members.
- Every legally permitted effort shall be made to secure humanity's deliverance from every type of exploitation, injustice, and oppression, and to ensure humanity's security, dignity, and liberty as set out in the law.

Right to Belief and Practicing One's Belief

- Every person is free to prefer a belief and practice it, although Islam has a right to be communicated to everyone in accordance with Allah's rules and the Messenger's practice. No one can be coerced to believe, not believe, or choose a certain belief.
- No one shall insult or ridicule the religious beliefs of others or incite public hostility against them, for all Muslims are obligated to respect the religious feelings of others.

Right to Life

- As human life is sacred and inviolable, every effort must be made to protect it. No one can be exposed to injury or death, unless the law permits it.
- Just as in life, so also after death the sanctity of a person's corpse shall be inviolable. Muslims must ensure that a deceased person's corpse is handled with due solemnity.

Right to Freedom

- Every person is born free. No inroads can be made upon his or her right to liberty, except under the authority of the law and due process.
- Every individual and people has the inalienable right to physical, cultural, economic, political, and all other types of freedom, and are entitled to struggle by all available means against any infringement or abrogation of this right. In addition, every oppressed individual or people has a legitimate claim upon the support of other individuals and peoples in such a struggle.

Right to Equality and Prohibition of Impermissible Discrimination

- All persons are equal before the law and are entitled to equal opportunity and its protection.
- All persons are entitled to equal wage for equal work.

- No person can be denied the opportunity to work, be discriminated against, or exposed to greater physical risk due to religious belief, color, race, origin, sex, or language.

Right to Justice

- Every person has the right to be treated in accordance with the law, and only in accordance with the law.
- Every person has the right and the obligation to protest injustice, to use any recourse to provided by the law to remedy any unwarranted personal injury or loss, to a defense against any charges laid against him or her, and to obtain fair adjudication before an independent judicial tribunal in any dispute with public authorities or with another person.
- Every person has the right and duty to defend the rights of any other person and the community in general (*hisba*).
- No person can be discriminated against while seeking to defend private and public rights.
- Every Muslim has the right to refuse to obey any command that is contrary to the law, no matter by whom it may be issued.

Right to a Fair Trial

- No person can be judged guilty of an offence and made liable to punishment before his or her guilt has been proven to an independent judicial tribunal.
- No person can be judged guilty before a fair trial and a reasonable opportunity for self-defense.
- Punishment shall be meted out in accordance with the law in proportion to the seriousness of the offence, and with due consideration of the surrounding circumstances.
- No act can be considered a crime, unless the law clearly stipulates it as such.
- Every individual is responsible for his or her actions. Responsibility for a crime cannot be placed upon other members of the

family or group, who are not directly or indirectly involved in the crime in question.

Right to Protection against the Abuse of Power

Every person has the right to protection against harassment by official agencies. A person is liable to account for himself or herself only when defending himself or herself against specific charges when there exists a reasonable suspicion of involvement.

Right to Protection against Torture

No person can be subjected to physical or mental torture; degraded; threatened either with personal injury or injury to his or her relatives or loved ones; made to confess to a crime; or forced to do something against his or her own will.

Right to Protection of Honor and Reputation

Every person has the right to protect his or her honor and reputation against calumny, groundless charges, or defamation and blackmail.

Right to Asylum

- Every persecuted or oppressed person has the right to seek refuge and asylum, irrespective of his or her race, religion, color, and sex.
- The Sacred Mosque (al-Masjid al-Haram) in Mecca is a sanctuary for all Muslims.

Rights of Minorities

- The Qur'anic principle of no compulsion in religion governs the religious rights of non-Muslim minorities.

- In a Muslim country, religious minorities have the choice to have their civil and personal matters governed by Islamic law or their own law.

Right and Obligation to Participate in Managing Public Affairs

- Subject to the law, every individual in the community is entitled to assume public office.
- Free consultation (*shura*) is the basis of the administrative relationship between the government and the people, and people can remove their rulers in accordance with it.

Right to the Freedom of Belief, Thought, and Speech

- Every person has the right to express his or her thoughts and beliefs so long as he or she remains within the law's limits. However, no one is entitled to disseminate falsehood, circulate reports that may outrage public decency, indulge in slander or innuendo, or defame others.
- The pursuit of knowledge and truth is a right and a duty of every Muslim.
- Every Muslim has the right and duty to protest and strive (within the law's limits) against oppression, even if it involves challenging the state's highest authority.
- There is no bar on disseminating information, provided it does not endanger the security of the society or the state, and is confined within the law's limits.

Right to Free Association

- Every person is entitled to participate, individually and collectively, in the community's religious, social, cultural, and political life, and to establish institutions and agencies that promote good and prevent evil.

- Every person is entitled to work to establish institutions that will allow these rights to be enjoyed. Collectively, the community is obliged to establish the conditions that will allow its members to fully develop their personalities.

The Economic Order and Related Rights

- All persons are entitled to the full benefits of nature and its resources to pursue their economic interests. These are blessings bestowed by Allah to benefit humanity as a whole.
- All people are entitled to earn their living according to the law.
- Every person is entitled to own property individually or in association with others. State ownership of certain economic resources in the public interest is legitimate.
- The poor have the right to a prescribed share in the wealth of the rich, as fixed by *Zakah* and levied and collected in accordance with the law.
- All means of production shall be used to benefit the community as a whole, and may not be neglected or misused.
- In order to promote the development of a balanced economy and to protect society from exploitation, Islamic law forbids monopolies, unreasonable restrictive trade practices, usury, coerced contracts, and publishing misleading advertisements.
- All economic activities are permitted, provided they do not harm the community's interests or violate Islamic laws and values.

Right to Protection of Property

No property may be expropriated, except by the law, in the public interest and on payment of fair and adequate compensation.

Status and Dignity of Workers

Islam honors work and the worker, and enjoins Muslims to treat workers justly and generously. They must be paid what they have earned promptly, and also entitled to adequate rest and leisure.

Right to Social Security

Every person has the right to food, shelter, clothing, education, and medical care consistent with the community's resources. This communal obligation extends in particular to all individuals who cannot take care of themselves due to some temporary or permanent disability.

Right to Establish a Family and Related Matters

- Every person is entitled to marry, establish a family, and bring up children in conformity with his or her religion, traditions, and culture. Every spouse is entitled to such rights and privileges, and carries such obligations as stipulated by the law.
- Each spouse is entitled to respect and consideration from the other spouse.
- Every husband is obligated to maintain his wife and children according to his means.
- Every child has the right to be maintained and properly brought up by his or her parents. Children cannot be made to work at an early age or bear any burden that might arrest or harm their natural development.
- If parents cannot discharge their obligations toward their children, the community must fulfill these obligations at public expense.
- Every person is entitled to material support, care, and protection from his or her family during childhood, old age, or incapacity. Parents are entitled to material support, care, and protection from their children.

- Motherhood is entitled to special respect, care, and assistance from the family and the community's public agencies.
- Within the family, men and women are to share in their obligations and responsibilities according to their gender, natural endowments, talents, and inclinations, bearing in mind their common responsibilities toward their progeny and relatives.
- No person may be married against his or her will, lose, or suffer a diminished legal personality on account of marriage.

Rights of Married Women

Every married woman is entitled to:

- live in the house in which her husband lives;
- receive what she needs to maintain a standard of living that is not inferior to that of her spouse, and, in the event of divorce, receive during her waiting period (*'idda*) support commensurate with her husband's resources both for herself and the children she nurses or keeps, irrespective of her own financial status, earnings, or property held in her own right;
- seek and obtain a dissolution of marriage in accordance with the law, as well as to seek a divorce through the courts;
- inherit from her husband, parents, children, and other relatives according to the law;
- strict confidentiality from her spouse, or ex-spouse if divorced, with regard to any personal information that, if made public, could harm her interests. Her husband or ex-husband also has similar rights over her.

Right to Education

- Every person is entitled to receive an education in accordance with his or her natural capability.

- Every person is entitled to freely choose his or her profession and career, and to the opportunity for full personal development.

Right to Privacy

Every person is entitled to the protection of privacy. Suspicion, spying, slandering, and backbiting are all forbidden.

Right to Freedom of Movement and Residence

- Every Muslim has the right to move freely in and out of Muslim lands.
- No one shall be forced to leave his or her country of residence or be deported arbitrarily without recourse to due process.

CHAPTER 2

HUMANITY: BETWEEN THE HIGHEST OF THE HIGH AND THE LOWEST OF THE LOW

HUMANITY: BETWEEN THE HIGHEST OF THE HIGH AND THE LOWEST OF THE LOW

THE ONTOLOGICAL NATURE OF HUMANKIND

The universe, an integral, composite entity all of whose parts are interrelated and interlinked with one another, may be likened to a tree. Particularly in Eastern traditions, it has been so likened and some Muslim sages have even written books on it under the title of "The Tree of Creation." It is Allah Almighty Who has created this Tree by manifesting His Names.

As everybody knows, a tree is grown from its seed or stone. The whole future life of the tree, the program of its life, is pre-recorded, compacted in the seed. The laws, such as the law of germination and the law of growth, which the Creator has established for the seed to germinate in propitious land and climate and grow into a tree, have the same meaning for the tree as the spirit has for a person. With the sowing of the seed in earth, the life of the tree proceeds through certain stages to yield its fruit and, having begun in a seed, ultimately ends in another seed which is almost identical with the original one and in which the whole past life of that tree is summed up.

Existential reality is almost the same in the whole of the universe as macro-cosmos, in humankind as normo-cosmos, and in an atom as micro-cosmos. Whatever Allah Almighty has included in the universe, He has compacted it in humankind's nature. So, being a specimen of creation, as Muslim sages tend to describe it, humankind, with its pure spiritual aspect, corresponds to angels; with the layers of its heart or spiritual intellect, to the pure, elevated, immaterial realms of existence; with its intellectual faculties, to the "seven heavens"; with its memory, to the Supreme Preserved Tablet where all things and events are pre-recorded and preserved both before and after they appear in the universe; with its bodily composition, to the main elements in nature; with its evil-commanding soul, to devils; and with its power, lusts and certain negative-seeming feelings and qualities requiring to be disciplined (like vindictiveness, cunning, deception, greed, rapaciousness, etc.) to certain animals, each of which is distinguished with one of these qualities.

Thus, humankind mainly has two aspects: one angelic, pure and spiritual; the other, turned to elements, plants and animals, as it is the "child of the world." It has been equipped with lusts to maintain its worldly life—lusts for the opposite sex, offspring, money, earning, and the comforts of life (See Qur'an, 3:14); with wrath or the power of anger to protect itself and its values; and with intellect. Besides, it is, by nature, fallible, forgetful, neglectful, fond of disputing, obstinate, selfish, jealous, and so forth. The Qur'an describes humankind with these two opposite aspects of its ontological nature as follows:

لَقَدْ خَلَقْنَا الْإِنْسَانَ فِي أَحْسَنِ تَقْوِيمٍ ۞ ثُمَّ رَدَدْنَاهُ أَسْفَلَ سَافِلِينَ

> Surely We have created human of the best stature, as the perfect pattern of creation; then We have reduced him to the lowest of the low. (95:4–5)

In another place, the Qur'an mentions the dual character of humankind with its sources as follows:

> Remember when your Lord said to the angels: "I am creating a mortal from dried, sounding clay, from molded dark mud. When I have fashioned him in due proportions and breathed into him out of My Spirit, then fall down prostrating before him (as a token of respect for him and his superiority)." (15:28–29)

The honor of humankind lies in our spiritual potential; this is what causes us to have the greatest rank among all created beings. Allah attributes it to Himself by saying, "My Spirit." The "spirit" is the source of life, both its physical and spiritual aspects, and therefore is not something material; rather, it is directly from Allah. Just as Allah Almighty mentions such ordinary things as earth, clay, and mud as being the material origin of humankind, and draws attention to the baseness of the material dimension of our existence, in order to present to view where the real value of humankind lies He mentions spirit and attributes it to Himself. This never means that Allah has a body and a spirit. Rather, it refers to humankind's sublime degree among created beings as of the best stature and the perfect pattern of creation, and where this degree lies. As explained above, the Almighty has created humankind as the manifestation of all of His Names which have given existence to the whole universe. This is why, unlike animals, human beings have consciousness, will-power, conscience, a well-developed power of learning, complex feelings, intellect, the power of reasoning, an ego or selfhood and ego-consciousness, and the feeling of freedom and independence.

HUMANKIND IN ITS RAW STATE—"THE LOWEST OF THE LOW"

Since humans are distinguished from other conscious beings like angels by being endowed with free will, which requires the preference between two opposite tendencies, and therefore responsibility, their powers, faculties and negative-seeming feelings have not been restricted in creation. However, in order to attain happiness as social beings, both in their individual and social life, in the world and in the Hereafter, and climb the steps of elevation to higher and higher ranks of humanity, they should either train and restrict their powers, faculties, and feelings according to certain precepts or channel them into virtues. For example, obstinacy can be channeled into steadfastness in right and truth, and jealousy into a feeling of competition in doing good things. True humanity lies in men's struggle against the negative aspects of their nature and restricting them or channeling them into virtues, and in their acquiring distinction with its good qualities, thus becoming good, worshipping servants of Allah and useful members of society. This is what the Last Prophet of Allah, upon him be peace and blessings, meant by saying, "I have been sent to perfect the standards and beauties of good morals."[1]

However, since, as mentioned above, Allah Almighty has reflected His Names and Attributes in the creation of humankind, or has created humankind as the theater where His Names and Attributes which have given existence to the universe are manifested one within the other, and since absolute Independence and Oneness or Uniqueness are the most essential Qualities of Divinity, human selfhood finds in itself a tendency towards individual independence. It imagines within itself a "fictitious" lordship, power, and knowledge. Allah has created it of this nature because through its imagined lordship, it can and must understand the absolute Lordship of the Creator of the universe; by means of its own apparent ownership, it can and must understand the real Ownership of its Creator; through its partial knowledge, willpower, and power, it can and must come to understand the Creator's absolute Knowledge, Will, and Power. For example, that selfhood can and must say, "I am the owner of this house of mine, so this universe must have an All-Powerful Owner. Seeing that it is not I who has created me, nourishes me, and has equipped me with the necessary instruments (bodily organs and faculties) to lead my life, it cannot be I who is the owner of my own self, and there must be One Who really owns me. My life requires that I must have certain degree of knowledge, will, and power, so the One Who owns me and the universe must have absolute Knowledge, Will, and Power." It can and must draw conclusions like these, and understand that its life-duty is to become a measure or a mirror to know and make known the Creator, Lord, and Owner of the universe with His Attributes and Names.

However, if, enamored of itself and deceived by its apparent lordship and ownership, human selfhood views itself as a self-existing being independent of the Creator, it betrays its life-duty or the purpose of its existence. It supposes itself to be a permanent reality which assumes that it owns its being and is the real lord and master of its own domain. Then, like some huge monster, it grows and swells until it gradually permeates the whole being of the person who has it. Eventually, the ego of the human race gives strength to the individual selfhood through mere individualism and national racism. This leads the selfhood to contest, like Satan, the Majestic Maker's commands. Finally, taking itself as a yardstick, it compares everyone and everything with itself, divides Allah's Sovereignty between them and other causes, and begins to associate partners with Allah in the most grievous manner. This development is responsible for all the varieties of polytheism, evil, and deviation in human history. The Qur'an describes this state of human selfhood as follows: *And he is indeed lost who has corrupted it (in self-aggrandizing and rebellion against Allah)* (91:10).

This betrayal of human selfhood causes it to sink into absolute ignorance. Even if it has absorbed thousands of branches of science, its ignorance is only compounded by its knowledge. Whatever glimmers of knowledge of Allah that it may have obtained from the universe through its senses or reflective powers have been extinguished, for it can no longer find within itself anything with which to confirm, polish, and maintain them. Whatever comes to it is stained with the colors within it. Even if pure wisdom comes, it becomes absolutely futile within the human selfhood stained by atheism, polytheism, or other forms of denying the All-Mighty. If the whole universe were full of shining indications of Allah, a dark point in that selfhood would hide them from view, as though they were invisible. The Qur'an describes this state of human selfhood:

> They have hearts with which they do not seek the essence of matters to grasp the truth, and they have eyes with which they do not see, and they have ears with which they do not hear. They are like cattle (following only their instincts)—rather, even more astray (from the right way and in need of being led). Those are the unmindful and heedless. (7:179)

> Have they never traveled about the earth (and viewed all these scenes of the past with an eye to learn lessons), so that they may have hearts with which to reason (and arrive at truth), or ears with which to hear (Allah's call)? For indeed, it is not the eyes that have become blind; it is rather the hearts in the breasts that are blind. (22:46)

HUMANKIND AND SATAN

Human spiritual development depends on humans' inner struggle with their evil-commanding souls and Satan. The motor of this struggle is the *willpower*, the basic mechanism which distinguishes humankind from angels and certain other beings such as animals and trees. Allah Almighty allowed Satan to attack humankind to mislead them so that in essence, humankind may be spiritually refined, develop, and rise to ever higher spiritual and moral stations. In order to succeed in the struggle against Satan, we should know how and from what fronts he attacks us. It is recounted in the Qur'an as follows:

> (*Iblis* [Satan]) continued: "Now that You have allowed me to rebel and go astray, I will surely lie in wait for them on Your Straight Path (to lure them from it). Then I will come upon them from before them and from behind them, and from their right and from their left. And You will not find most of them thankful." (7:16–17)

Satan's attacks upon humankind from their four sides have been explained as follows:

> I will come upon them from before them, and sow in them worry and hopelessness concerning their future; I will invite them not to pay the *Zakah* or do any supererogatory forms of charity in fear of becoming poor; I will urge them to hoard their wealth; I will provoke them to disbelieve in the Hereafter and show them a dark future; I will present to them the way of the Prophets as reactionary and regressive; and I will call them into valleys of misguidance through the promises I make to them about their future.
>
> I will come upon them from behind them, and show them the past as a dark cemetery; and by showing them both the past and the present as dark, I will drive them to pessimism and distress after distress; I will incite them to turn away from the way of the Prophets, and to condemn and reject their past while following this way, encouraging them to revive their former (ancient) past, when they worshipped many so-called deities and lived a corrupt life of sheer ignorance, and to see all this as progress.

I will come upon them from their right and show them their religious devotions as being perfect, driving them to ostentation, self-pride, and to the desire that their religious life be known and praised by others, thereby causing all their good deeds to go to waste. I will also provoke them to attach more importance to secondary matters in religion, while neglecting the essentials, thus provoking them to disagree and causing conflict. Again, I will cause them to use religion for their worldly interests and ambitions, and for the satisfaction of their carnal desires, but will whisper to them that they do so for the sake of religion, and try my best in order that they may go to the Hereafter devoid of any good deeds.

I will come upon them from their left, and incite them to reject Allah's Existence, the Hereafter, and other essentials of faith, and to search different systems of belief or ideology; I will urge them to struggle and even fight against Allah's religion and those who follow it; I will invite them to dive into the swamp of sins, such as adultery, prostitution, drinking alcohol, and gambling and similar games of chance; I will provoke them to unlawful transactions, like bribery, usury, corruption, theft, robbery, and deception, and other forms of wrong, such as injustice, oppression, murder, disrespect to parents, and the violation of basic human rights, and I will call them to present all these under the titles of justice, peace, humanism, progress, and civilization, and so on.

THE MOST OBSERVABLE CHARACTERISTICS OF HUMAN SELFHOOD AS "THE LOWEST OF THE LOW"

The Qur'an mentions the most observable characteristics of human selfhood in betrayal of its life-duty mentioned above or as "the lowest of the low" as follows:

Rebellious and Ungrateful to Their Lord

No, indeed (despite all His favors to him), human is unruly and rebels, in that he sees himself as self-sufficient, independent (of his Lord). (96:6–7)

Surely human is ungrateful to his Lord. And to this, he him-self is a sure witness; and most surely he is violent in love of wealth. (100:6–8)

Prone to Selfish Avarice and Ever Grudging

(Bear in mind that) human souls are prone to selfish avarice. (4:128)

Say: "If you possessed the treasures of my Lord's Mercy, still you would surely hold them back for fear of spending (in Allah's cause, and as subsistence for the needy)." Indeed human is ever grudging. (17:100)

Have you considered one who denies the Last Judgment? That is he who repels the orphan, and does not urge the feeding of the destitute. (107:1–3)

But as for him who is niggardly and regards himself as self-suffi-cient in independence of Him, and denies the best (in creed, action, and the reward to be given): We will make easy for him the path to hardship (punishment after a hard reckoning). And his wealth will not avail him when he falls to ruin. (92:8–11)

Plunging in Self-Indulgence and Lost in the Playthings of the Worldly Life

The basic aim of uneducated souls in worldly life is the gratification of their worldly appetites. They plunge in self-indulgence and are lost in the diversions of the worldly life:

Allah has promised the hypocrites, both men and women, and the unbelievers, the fire of Hell, therein to abide: it is (recom-pense) to suffice them. Allah has excluded them from His mercy, and for them is a lasting punishment, just like the peo-ples before you (O hypocrites and unbelievers) who were greater than you in power and more abundant in wealth and children. They enjoyed their lot (in the world) for a while, and you have been enjoying your lot, just as those who preceded you enjoyed their lot; and you have plunged in self-indulgence, as others who plunged. Such (hypocrites and unbelievers) are those whose works have been wasted in both this world and the Hereafter, and those—they are the losers. (9:68–69)

Yet (they do not desire certainty; instead) they are in an irrecoverable doubt, lost in the playthings of the worldly life. (44:9)

Woe, then, on that Day to those who deny (Allah's Message and the Messengers)—Those who are habitually playing, absorbed (in vanities): on that Day, they will be forcefully thrust into the fire of Hell. (52:11–13)

Following Conjecture, not Knowledge

And if you pay heed to the majority of those on the earth, they will lead you astray from Allah's way. They follow only conjecture (not knowledge), and they themselves do nothing but make guesses (they pronounce and act according to their fancies, selfish interests, and personal value judgments). (6:116)

They have no knowledge of this. They follow nothing other than conjecture, and conjecture can never substitute for anything of the truth. (53:28)

Thankless and Self-Glorifying

If We let human taste some mercy from Us, and then take it away from him, he becomes hopeless and thankless (forgetting all Our favors to him). And if We let him taste ease and plenty after some hardship has visited him, he says: "Gone is all affliction from me!" Surely he is prone to vain exultation and self-glorifying. (11:9–10)

The Qur'an gives the example of two people, one a humble believer, and the other selfish and conceited, about whom the Qur'an relates:

He went into his vineyard while wronging himself (in his vain conceit). He said: "I do not think that this will ever perish. Nor do I think that the Last Hour will ever come. Even if (it should come, and) I am brought back to my Lord, I will surely find something even better than this as a resort." His companion said to him, while he was arguing with him: "Do you (expressing such ingratitude) disbelieve in Him Who created you from earth, then out of a mere drop of seminal fluid, then fashioned you into a perfect man? But (for my part I believe that) He is Allah, my Lord, and I do not associate with my Lord any partner. If only you had said, on entering your vineyard, 'Whatever Allah wills (surely has and surely will come to pass); there is no strength (to achieve anything) save with Allah.'" (18:35–39).

The mood of the selfish, conceited unbeliever is typical of many worldly people. They attribute whatever they have in the world to themselves. Because of this, they do not like anyone else, for example, the poor and the needy, to have any share in it. They are so puffed up by their worldly things that they deceive themselves into believing that Allah is their Lord in particular, and He is ready to welcome them under any circumstances. Such people are usually ignorant upstarts with crude manners.

Prone to Wrongdoing, Misjudging, and Ignorant

He has granted you from all that you ask Him. Were you to attempt to count Allah's blessings, you could not compute them. But for sure, humankind is much prone to wrongdoing (sins and errors of judgment) and to ingratitude. (14:34)

Human is indeed prone to doing great wrong and misjudging, and acting out of sheer ignorance. (33:72)

A Disputant and Adversary

He has created human from (so slight a beginning as) a mere drop of seminal fluid; and yet, he turns into an open, fierce adversary (selfishly disputing against the truth). (16:4)

Has man not considered that We have created him from (so slight a beginning as) a drop of (seminal) fluid? Yet, he turns into an open, fierce adversary (selfishly disputing against the truth). (36:77)

Adoring Their Lusts and Fancies

Do you ever consider him who has taken his lusts and fancies for his deity? Would you then be a guardian over him (and, thereby, assume responsibility for guiding him)? (25:43)

Do you ever consider him who has taken his lusts and fancies for his deity, and whom Allah has (consequently) led astray though he has knowledge (of guidance and straying), and sealed his hearing and his heart, and put a cover on his sight? Who, then, can guide him after Allah (has led him astray)? Will you not then reflect and be mindful? (45:23)

Deifying one's lusts and fancies means pursuing one's lusts and fancies at all costs and making the satisfaction of them the goal of one's life. The greatest obstacle to believing in Allah or being attached to His Religion is one's carnal soul prompting one to pursue the satisfaction of lusts, whether lawfully or unlawfully. Allah's Messenger, upon him be peace and blessings, warned, "Of all the false deities that are worshipped under the sky, the worst in Allah's sight is one's carnal, evil-commanding soul."[2]

Hopeless in the Face of Calamities; Self-Glorifying and Self-Centered in the Face of Favors

In several of its verses, the Qur'an draws attention to the fact that humans, particularly those who have no sound belief in Allah and the afterlife, become desperate in the face of calamities visiting them, but exult in the favors they receive and begin associating partners with Allah. For example:

Whatever blessing you have, it is from Allah; and when harm touches you, it is to Him that you cry for help. When, thereafter, He removes the harm from you, a party of you attribute partners to their Lord (Who alone sustains and provides for you, and saves you from misfortunes); and so deny with ingratitude the favors Allah has granted them. (16:53–55)

> When We favor human (an ungrateful one) with comfort and contentment, he draws aside and arrogantly keeps aloof (from any thought of Us); but when evil touches him, he is ever despairing. (17:83)

> When an affliction befalls human, he calls upon his Lord turning to Him (in contrition); then when He bestows a favor upon him, he forgets what he prayed to Him for before, and sets up rivals to Allah so that he (himself goes astray and) misleads (others) from His way. (39:8)

> When an affliction befalls human, he calls upon Us (to save him). Then, when We (from sheer grace) have bestowed a favor upon him from Us, he says: "I have been given this only by virtue of a certain knowledge that I have." No, indeed. Rather, this (favor bestowed on human) is a trial, but most of them do not know. (39:49)

> Human never tires of asking for (what he presumes is) his own good, but if evil befalls him, then he gives up all hope and loses heart. (41:49).

This is typical of one who does not believe in Allah as the Creator of all good and evil, and in Divine Destiny. Since such persons concentrate on worldly life in pursuit of its enjoyments, and attribute everything to their own knowledge and abilities according to the "law" of cause and effect, when they feel that there is no longer any means to attain something, they become utterly desperate. In contrast, a believer never loses hope because he or she believes that it is Allah Who also creates the means to attain something, and He can always create new means when one fails. Believers also know for certain that Allah is the Creator of all things, including good and evil, and that evil is an outcome of their own choices. So when they cannot attain something, they either think that they have made a mistake in trying to attain it, or that Allah does not will them to have it because it is not good for them to attain it.

Accusing Allah and Having Extreme
Love of Wealth and Hoarding

And so, human—when his Lord tries him by bestowing favors on him—says: "My Lord has honored me." But whenever He tries him by straitening his means of livelihood, then he says, "My Lord has humiliated me." No indeed! You (O people) do not treat the orphan with kindness and generosity; and do not urge one another to feed the destitute; and you consume inheritance (belonging to you or others) with greed (without distinction of the lawful and unlawful); and you love wealth with a boundless ardor for it and for hoarding. (89:15–20)

Given to Contention

Assuredly We have set out in diverse ways for humankind in this Qur'an all kinds of parables and comparisons (to help them understand the truth); but humankind is, above all else, given to contention. (18:54)

Insistent on Following Their Wrong Way
or Blind Imitation

The Qur'an frequently warns against blind insistence on following the wrong way due to some factors such as imitation of the forefathers. For example:

Now recite to them this exemplary account of Abraham. When he said to his father and his people: "What is it that you worship?" They said: "We worship idols; and (even though they are made of wood and stone) we are ever devoted to them (as they are our deities)." (Abraham) said: "Do they hear you when you invoke them? Or do they benefit you (when you worship them), or harm (you when you do not)?" They replied: "But we found our forefathers doing the same." (26:69–75)

This is typical human nature. It is really very difficult for human beings to abandon established ideas and customs. People tend not to think too much about whether or not what they are doing is rational or is based on some truth. Islam brings freedom to human thinking, saves the human mind from prejudice and blind imitation, and explains the truth in all its clarity, aiming at removing all obstacles that can be placed before free human choice. A. Cressy Morrison, former head of the New York Academy of Sciences, drawing attention to this aspect of human nature, says, "The early Greeks knew the earth was a sphere, but it took two thousand years to convince (Western) men that this fact is true. New ideas encounter opposition, ridicule and abuse, but truth survives and is verified."[3]

Following the Religion in Expectation of Only Worldly Gains

Many worldly people, even though they seemingly follow the Divine Religion and worship Allah, pursue worldly benefits:

> Among people are also many a one who worships Allah on the borderline (of faith), in expectation of only worldly gains. If any good befalls him, he is satisfied with it, but if a trial afflicts him, he turns away utterly, reverting back to unbelief. He (thereby) incurs loss of both this world and the Hereafter. This indeed is the obvious loss. (22:11)

Preferring the Worldly Life to the Hereafter

One of the primary reasons for misguidance is that humans tend to prefer the immediate pleasures of the worldly life to the happiness of the afterlife. This is because humans are impatient and addicted to immediate gain. The Qur'an frequently warns humankind against this tendency:

> But you (O humans) are disposed to prefer the life of this world, while the Hereafter is better and more lasting. (87:16–17)

> Allah, to Whom belongs whatever is in the heavens and whatever is on the earth; and woe to the unbelievers because of a severe punishment. They choose the present, worldly life in preference to the Hereafter, and bar (people) from Allah's way, and seek to make it appear crooked—those have indeed gone far astray. (14:2–3)

Restless and Impatient

> Yet human (through his actions as well as his words) prays and calls for evil just as he prays and calls for good. Human is prone to be hasty. (17:11)

Unless Allah informs us, we cannot know what is ultimately to our advantage and what is to our disadvantage. The Qur'an declares, *It may well be that you dislike a thing but it is good for you, and it may well be that you like a thing but it is bad for you. Allah knows, and you do not know* (2:216). For this reason, many people usually desire and call down on themselves (by their words and actions) what is evil for them, thinking that it is for their own good. They even pray to Allah for evil, knowingly or unknowingly, under the spell of their carnal souls and worldly ambitions. As mentioned above, they also desire what they think of as an advance payment, and dislike what they think of as a payment on credit. This is why they usually prefer a worldly advantage over eternal reward in the Hereafter, which is one of the primary reasons for their errors, including unbelief. This is mostly because people are disposed to haste. Humans are, by nature, hasty. Like other apparently negative attributes, such as greed, envy, and obstinacy, this attribute is ingrained in people so that they may channel it into virtues. The Messenger, upon him be peace and blessings, declares that hastiness comes from Satan. However, he also advises that we should not postpone doing good, and we should show celerity in good things, such as doing the Prescribed Prayers on time and helping the needy.

Nine Vices in a Person

There may even be people stained with ten vices, as the Qur'an mentions:

> Pay no heed to any frequent oath-maker, contemptible; a defamer, circulating slander (in all directions), who hinders the doing of good; a transgressor of all bounds (of sense or decency); one addicted to sinning, cruel and ignoble; and in addition to all that, morally corrupt. (68:10–13)

THE PERFECTIBILITY OF HUMANITY

The materialistic point of view restricts human existence to our physical aspect only and regards all the metaphysical aspects of our existence as derivative from our physical aspect. However, it is plainly seen that we, as human beings, are such complex beings with such comprehensive faculties, desires and feelings that it is impossible to attribute the metaphysical dimension of our existence to deaf, blind, ignorant, unconscious and inert matter. Despite our resemblance in physical structure, our essential needs and their ways and means of satisfaction, and the source of our physical being, we are worlds apart from each other in character, each of us having a different individuality and being a different world. In imagination we can traverse in a few seconds the whole realm of material existence and go beyond it. Our feelings and desires are not restricted to the physical world; they extend beyond it. We love and hate, pity and cherish enmity and vengeance, are pleased and dissatisfied, rejoice and are grieved, and so on. These and other similar feelings all have different and lasting effects upon us.

Also, we have a special relation with our environment, our relatives, other human beings, animals, and the whole of nature. Just as the whole life history and features of a tree end or are included in its fruit, so too we, as the fruit of the tree of creation, contain in our being all the principal aspects or features of existence. This feature of our being must be considered in our relations with our natural environment; the neglect of it in modern times is the basic reason for modern environmental problems.

Another point to note concerning our existence is that we have been endowed with free will and great potentialities which can be continually expanded through learning and practice, and that the Creator did not restrict our drives or faculties. For example, the Creator put no limits upon our three cardinal powers, namely those of anger, lust and reason or intellect. The power of anger is the origin of our instincts of defense: the power of desire is the source of our animal appetites, among them the urge to have relations with the opposite sex; the power of reason or intellect is the center of our mental activities. We may note also that we carry in our being the main characteristics of every animal. For example, we can be as rapacious as a wolf, and as cunning and deceiving as a fox.

If we let our powers drive us and obey their demands, and if we do not discipline our animal characteristics, then these powers and characteristics can become the source of innumerable vices. If undisciplined, our power of anger can cause great crimes such as murder, all kinds of injustices and violations of others' rights; the power of desire can lead us to consume whatever we find, to earn in any way we find convenient, to commit many crimes such as theft and fraud, to have illicit sexual relations and seek to hide the consequences with abortion and infanticide. The power of reason, if it is not used according to certain standards, can be a means for such deceitful practices as demagogy, lying and sophistry. This power which has enabled us to realize admirable scientific and technological successes and developments in recent centuries, has also brought us many disasters unparalleled in human history such as continual wars, machines for killing and destruction on an unbelievable scale, and increasing environmental pollution. In short, because our powers are unrestricted in creation, we, if undisciplined, can be an agent of destruction and make life and the world into a dungeon for ourselves. Therefore, all of our powers and faculties need training or education. According to what standards must we train them?

In addition, we are social beings, compelled to live together with our fellow beings. Harmonious social life requires justice and mutual helping which is only possible by our conformity to certain rules or standards of conduct. Necessarily, these rules must restrict our desires and drives. Since our essential needs and characters have remained stable since our appearance on the earth, these rules and standards must be universal and stable and applicable to all human beings in all times and places. Seeing that we are even unable to discover ourselves and "man remains to be a being unknown," it is highly questionable whether we can know what and of what character both these rules and standards and the standards according to which we must train our powers and faculties must be. It is a plain fact that it is almost impossible for even two people to agree on all points. If the task of establishing the rules and standards in question were given to one individual or to one family or to one class or to one nation or to those with enough power to put them into effect and force others to obey, the consequence must inevitably be injustice and inequality among people. Therefore, a universal or transcendent intellect is necessary. Such an intellect can only be derived from Allah, as manifested in the Religion revealed by the Creator of all existence, Who knows all things, internally and externally, from the largest to the smallest, and all their interconnections from before to after time. However, since it is impossible for every human being individually to receive Divine Revelation, Allah Almighty chose some persons among human beings (the Prophets and Messengers, upon them be peace) and charged them to convey His Religion to people. After the Last Prophet, upon him be peace and blessings, no one and no institution has the right to be an intermediary between Allah and human beings in receiving and conveying His Religion. Only those who are well-versed in religious sciences can offer authoritative guidance for others concerning the problems people may encounter. By obeying God-established rules or standards, we can restrain our powers in a way that will result in our finding happiness and in justice and equity among people.

All these facts discussed about our existence lead us to think about the purpose of our existence, concerning which Said Nursi writes as follows:

> The highest aim of creation and its most sublime result is belief in Allah. The most exalted rank of humanity is the knowledge of Allah. The most radiant happiness and sweetest bounty for humankind is the love of Allah issuing from the knowledge of Allah. The purest joy for the human spirit and the purest delight for the human heart is the spiritual ecstasy contained within the love of Allah. Indeed, all true happiness, pure joy,

sweet bounties and unclouded pleasures are undoubtedly contained within the knowledge and love of Allah. The one who knows and loves Allah is either potentially or actually able to receive endless happiness, favors, enlightenment, and understanding. While the one who does not truly know and love Him is afflicted spiritually and materially by endless misery, pain and fear. Indeed, even if a person, powerless and miserable, and unprotected amid other purposeless human beings in a world filled with wretchedness, were made the ruler of the whole world, what would this really be worth for him?[4]

Another important point to note concerning our existence and essential nature is the difference between us and animals. While animals only experience the moment, without suffering either from the misfortunes of the past or worries about the future, the pains coming from past misfortunes and the anxieties we feel about our future never leave us. Our needs are infinite, and so are our desires and ambitions. Secondly, almost from the very moment an animal is born, it seems to have been sent to this world having been trained in another, perfected in all its faculties. Within a few hours or days or months, it comes into full possession of its natural capacity to lead its life according to particular rules and conditions. A sparrow or a bee, for example, acquires, or, rather, is inspired with, the skill and ability to integrate into its environment in a matter of twenty days; for a human to achieve the same level of skill requires twenty years.

By contrast, we are born with no knowledge of life or our environment, and with a need to learn everything. Unable to entirely complete the conditions of life, even after twenty years, we need to continue learning until the end of our life. We come or rather are sent to the world with much weakness and inability; it may even take us one year or so to learn just how to walk. Only after fifteen years can we distinguish between what is harmful and want is beneficial for us.

Drawing attention to this important point, Said Nursi remarks as follows:

An animal's basic obligation and essential role does not include seeking perfection through learning, progress through scientific knowledge, or prayer and petitioning for help by displaying its impotence. Rather, its sole purpose is to act within the bounds of its innate faculties, which is the mode of worship specified for it.

However, the essential and intrinsic duty of our existence is to seek perfection through learning and to proclaim our worship of and servanthood to Allah through prayer and supplication. We should seek answers for: "Through whose compassion is my life so wisely administered? Through whose generosity am I being so affectionately trained? Through whose favors and benevolence am I being so solicitously nourished?" and other questions. Then we should pray and petition the Provider of Needs in humble awareness of our needs, none of which we can satisfy on our own. This understanding and confession of impotence and poverty will become two wings on which to fly to the highest rank: being a servant of Allah.[5]

Our basic powers, desires and faculties have been given to us so that we should use them within certain bounds and make them the sources of certain virtues. For example, we are not expected to eradicate our lust, rather we should satisfy it in lawful ways and use it as a means of reproduction. Thus, our happiness, which has always been one of the primary subjects discussed by social sciences and psychology, lies, as well as in belief in and knowledge and love of Allah, in our training and restraining our powers. Belief in and love of Allah also require this training and restraint. We must train our lust and restrain it within the lawful bounds of decency and chastity, without indulgence in debauchery and dissipation. Our power of anger has been given to us so that we may use it in defense of our sacred values and basic rights and freedoms—the Religion, intellect, life, private property, and having a family and reproduction—against attacks. That is, we must not use it unlawfully to exploit and oppress or injure and kill others. Therefore, it requires that we must train it and restrain it within the legal bounds required by our basic rights and duties towards the Creator, other people, and the natural environment. Also, virtuous direction in the exercise of reason is understanding, wisdom and truthfulness. Reason must not be used to deceive others for selfish advantage.

We also have certain feelings which are intrinsic to our nature, such as jealousy, hatred, enmity, hypocrisy and ostentation. If such feelings are not trained and directed to virtue, they consume us. For example, jealousy must be channeled into emulation free of rancor, which inspires us to imitate those who excel us in goodness and good deeds. Hatred and enmity should be directed primarily against our own carnal souls and the bad aspects of our character. As for hypocrisy and ostentation, we must try to be rid of them. If that is impossible for us, we should at least try to make show of only the better sides of our character and compete with others in virtuous deeds.

In addition to training and restricting our powers and certain feelings and tendencies, our happiness requires the satisfaction of all aspects of our existence. Made of dust (our earthly element), intellect, and spirit (our heavenly element), we have to satisfy our material, intellectual, and spiritual needs. Just as our physical body is subject to its own pleasures and diseases, our intellect and spirit each has its own joys and ailments. Sickness harms the body, while the body's well-being, health, and whatever is in harmony with its nature gives it pleasure. While our intellect finds satisfaction in knowledge based on knowledge of Allah, our spirit finds rest and contentment in the remembrance of and whole-hearted devotion to Allah. Concerning this essential aspect of our existence and source of happiness, Said Nursi writes as follows:

> The human conscious nature, which we call conscience, which feels pleasure and exhilaration in what is good, and suffers from and is grieved by what is evil, consists of four basic elements, namely the spiritual intellect, willpower, the mind, and the power of perceptiveness. These four elements are also regarded as the senses of the spirit. In addition to their different duties and functions, each of these senses has an ultimate purpose for its existence. The ultimate purpose for willpower is worshipping Allah; for the mind, it is having knowledge of Allah; for the power of perceptiveness, it is the love of Allah; for the

spiritual intellect, it is the vision of Allah. What we call *taqwa* (piety and righteousness), which is the perfect form or degree of worship, is the result of the functions of all four senses. The Divine Religion feeds them so that they develop, equips them with the necessary material, and directs them to the ultimate purposes for the existence of each.[6]

Servanthood to Allah never reduces us. By contrast, it elevates us. In human history from Adam's time until the present, two great currents or lines of thought have spread their branches in all directions and in every class of humanity, just like two tall trees. One is the line of Prophethood and Religion, which requires and has established servanthood to Allah or worshipping Him; the other is that of mere human thinking. Whenever they have agreed and united (whenever human thinking joins the Religion in obedience and service to it), humankind has experienced brilliant happiness in individual and collective life. But whenever they have followed separate paths, truth and goodness have generally accumulated on the side of Prophethood and the Religion, whereas error, evil, and deviation have been drawn to the side of human thinking.

Prophethood considers that the aim and function of human beings is to be molded by Divine values and to achieve good character. Prophets believed that people should perceive their weakness, and seek refuge in the Divine Power and rely on Divine Strength; realize their insufficiency and essential poverty, and trust in Divine Mercy; know their need and seek help from Divine Wealth; see their faults and plead for pardon through Divine Forgiveness; and perceive their inadequacy and glorify Divine Perfection.

According to human thinking that has deviated, power is approved. "Might is right" is the norm. Its maxims are: "All power to the strongest"; "Survival of the fittest"; "Winner takes all"; and, "In power, there is right." It has usually given moral support to tyranny, encouraged dictators, and urged oppressors to claim Divinity. By ascribing the beauty and accomplishments in "works of art" or in creation to the works themselves, and not to the Absolute Maker and Fashioner, it says, "How beautiful it is!"; "How successful it is!" and not, "How beautifully it is made!"; "What wonders Allah wills!" and thus considers each as an idol worthy of adoration.

Also, among Prophethood's fundamental principles of social life are mutual assistance, magnanimity, and generosity. These function in the reciprocal cooperation of all things—from the sun and the moon down to particles. For example, plants help animals, animals help people, and particles of food help the body's cells. Human irreligious thinking, however, considers conflict to be the fundamental condition of social life. In fact, conflict springs from tyrants, brutes, and savage people misusing their innate dispositions. Conflict is so fundamental and general to the irreligious human thinking that they absurdly claim that "life is conflict."[7]

Sincere servants of Allah are worshipping servants, but ones who never degrade themselves to bow in adoration or humiliation even before the greatest of the created. They are dignified servants who do not regard as the goal of worship a thing of even the greatest benefit like Paradise. Also, they are modest, mild and gentle, but they do not lower themselves voluntarily before anybody other than their Creator beyond what He has permitted. They may also be weak and in want, and be aware of their essential weakness and neediness. Yet they are independent of others, owing to the spiritual wealth which their Munificent Owner has provided for them, and they are powerful as they rely on the infinite Power of their Master. They act and strive purely for Allah's sake, for Allah's good pleasure, and to be equipped with virtues.[8]

To be a good, virtuous servant of Allah Almighty and thereby find true happiness, we must oppose our carnal, evil-commanding soul and fight against it so as always to use our willpower in the correct way. Life finds its true meaning through this struggle, evolves, and is perfected. The pleasure of this struggle lies in itself. It is like climbing an upward path. Walking on leveled surfaces does not give us any pleasure, but when those who continuously climb hills or walk an uphill road reach the summit and wipe the sweat from their forehead, they experience the great pleasure of achievement. But for winter, spring would not be so beautiful. So, our true happiness and the real pleasure of life lie in our struggle against the temptations of our carnal, evil-commanding soul and Satan and becoming victorious against both. This is how we can rise along the path of perfectibility towards the heavens, towards endless and eternal happiness and pleasures, towards being truly human and recovering our state as the best pattern of creation and eternal inhabitant of Paradise.

KHILAFA OR VICEGERENCY ON THE EARTH

In several of its chapters (e.g., *Surat al-Baqara* and *Surat al-Hijr*), the Qur'an relates the creation and deployment of humankind on the earth as *khalifa* or vicegerent. The relevant verses in the *Surat al-Baqara* read as follows:

> Remember (when) your Lord said to the angels: "I am setting on the earth a vicegerent." The angels asked: "Will you set therein one who will cause disorder and corruption on it and shed blood, while we glorify You with Your praise (proclaiming that You are absolutely free from any defect and that all praise belongs to You exclusively,) and declare that You alone are All-Holy and to be worshipped as Allah and Lord?" He said: "Surely I know what you do not know." (Having brought him into existence,) Allah taught Adam the names, all of them. Then (in order to clarify the supremacy of humankind and the wisdom in their being created and made vicegerent on the earth), He presented them (the things and beings, whose names had been taught to Adam, with their names) to the angels, and said, "Now tell Me the names of these, if you are truthful (in your praising, worshipping, and sanctifying Me as My being Allah and Lord deserves). (In acknowledgement of their imperfection, and their perception of the truth of the matter,) the angels said: "All-Glorified You are (in that You are absolutely above having any defect and doing anything meaningless, and Yours are all the attributes of perfection). We have no knowledge save what You have taught us. Surely You are the All-Knowing, the All-Wise." (In order to demonstrate the superiority of humankind more clearly,) Allah said: "O Adam, inform

them of these things and beings with their names." When he (Adam) informed them with their names, He said (to the angels), "Did I not tell you that I know the unseen of the heavens and the earth, and I know all that you reveal and all that you have been concealing?" And (remember) when We said to the angels: "Prostrate before Adam!" they all prostrated, but Iblis did not; he refused, and grew arrogant, and displayed himself as an unbeliever. "O Adam! Dwell you, and your spouse, in the Garden, and eat (of the fruits) thereof to your hearts' content where you desire, but do not approach this tree, or you will both be among the wrongdoers." But Satan (tempting them to the forbidden tree despite Our forewarning,) caused them both to deflect therefrom and brought them out of the (happy) state in which they were. And We said, "Go down, all of you, (and henceforth you will live a life,) some of you being the enemies of others. There shall be for you on the earth a habitation and provision until an appointed time." (Aware of his lapse and in the hope of retrieving his error, rather than attempting to find excuses for it,) Adam received from his Lord words that he perceived to be inspired in him (because of his remorse, and he pleaded through them for Allah's forgiveness). In return, He accepted his repentance. He is the One Who accepts repentance and returns it with liberal forgiveness and additional reward, the All-Compassionate (especially towards His believing servants). (2:30–37)

The primary reason why humankind was accorded superiority over the angels is that we were "taught the names." The duty of humankind on the earth is vicegerency or *khilafa*, literally meaning succession. According to some interpreters of the Qur'an, this indicates another species or kind of beings on the earth preceding humankind. These were the jinn, who were succeeded by humankind because of their unending conflicts and revolts against Allah.

As a term, *khilafa* or vicegerency denotes improving the earth, on the basis of knowledge of things and the laws of creation (which modern science calls the "laws of nature"), and ruling on the earth according to the dictates of Allah, thus establishing justice. Carrying out this duty requires scientific knowledge and the Religion. Humankind can acquire scientific knowledge by studying nature and is given the Religion through Allah's Messengers. The Books given or revealed to the Messengers, in addition to containing the religious principles, are, in one respect, like discourses describing nature and its meaning. That is why, in Islam, the universe, or nature, is seen as the "Created Book," and its laws as the laws of the creation and operation of the universe issuing from the Divine Attributes of Will and Power. The Qur'an is the "Revealed Book," the set of Divine laws and principles issuing from Allah's Attribute of Speech. For this reason, there can and should be no dichotomy or conflict between science and the Religion.

The names taught to Adam are the names of both things and his descendants. We know this from the use of the pronoun *hum*—meaning "their" in the compound "their names" in verse 33 above—which is used for conscious beings. It shows that Adam's descendants are included among the "names" taught to him. The angels must have fully comprehended Adam's supremacy and the wisdom in his vicegerency, not merely because of his being taught the names that they had not been taught, but also because they saw the illustrious members of humankind among the descendants of Adam—such as the Prophets, saints, and pure, exacting scholars, who would change the earth into gardens of Paradise through their faith, knowledge and morality.

The knowledge of things was given to Adam in summarized form and then, during the course of history, was taught to the Messengers in relative detail according to the mission of each. That is why the Messengers became also the forerunners of scientific knowledge and progress, in addition to their being guides in spirituality and morality. The Qur'an, which is the consummation of all the previous Scriptures, sheds light on future scientific studies and discoveries, and indicates their final point of advancement in its narrations of the miracles of the Messengers.[9]

The names taught to Adam also signify the potential for learning bestowed on humankind. Giving a name means knowing, for one can give a name only to something one knows. As explained above, animals come, or rather, are sent, to the world as if taught and trained in another world. They are adapted to the conditions of their life within a very short period as if they knew them already. By contrast, it takes human beings, on average, one year to learn how to walk, and many more years to learn the conditions of life, to distinguish securely between what is harmful and what is beneficial for them. This learning indeed continues until death, as evidence that learning has a fundamental place in human life and progress.

As pointed out above, vicegerency denotes humankind's ruling on the earth and improving it by using all that is subjected to it in accordance with the dictates of Allah. We have stated above that if humans attribute to themselves what Allah has given them of knowledge, power, the ability to learn, and various other capacities, and then attempt to act independently of Allah, it is then that disorder and bloodshed begin on the earth. For this reason, we should emphasize once more that their happiness, dignity, and the improvement of the earth lie in acknowledging their innate weakness, poverty, and ignorance before Allah and thus finding and depending on the only and infinite source of Power, Sufficiency and Knowledge.

CHAPTER 3

CERTAIN VIRTUES ENCOURAGED IN THE QUR'AN AND THE SUNNA

CERTAIN VIRTUES ENCOURAGED IN THE QUR'AN AND THE SUNNA

In many of its verses, the Qur'an draws attention to certain virtues either by way of commands or encouragement. Also, Allah's Messenger, upon him be peace and blessings, either explains them or tells us about their importance, and calls us to equip ourselves with them. It should be borne in mind that those virtues are both the fruits and standards of good, sincere Islamic belief, worship, and life. Many of these virtues are as follows:

SINCERITY OR PURITY OF INTENTION

Intention is the spirit of acts and changes the nature of things. As an elixir, it turns soil into gold; good intention and correct viewpoint change evil acts into good ones. Intention transforms our everyday, ordinary acts into acts of worship. Acceptance of our religious acts depends on our sincerity or purity of intention. It is because of this that Imam al-Bukhari preferred the *hadith* concerning intention as the first *hadith* in his *al-Jami' as-Sahih*, his illustrious compendium where he recorded the accurately related *hadith*s:

> Deeds are evaluated according to the intentions for them, and every person gets but what he has intended. So whoever emigrated for worldly benefits or for a woman to marry, his emigration is for what he emigrated for.

The Qur'an relates to us the experience of two sons of Adam about being able or unable to draw near to Allah, and indicates the importance of sincerity in intention and true piety for Allah's acceptance of good deeds:

وَاتْلُ عَلَيْهِمْ نَبَأَ ابْنَيْ اٰدَمَ بِالْحَقِّ إِذْ قَرَّبَا قُرْبَانًا فَتُقُبِّلَ مِنْ أَحَدِهِمَا وَلَمْ يُتَقَبَّلْ مِنَ الْاٰخَرِ قَالَ لَأَقْتُلَنَّكَ قَالَ إِنَّمَا يَتَقَبَّلُ اللهُ مِنَ الْمُتَّقِينَ

Narrate to them (O Messenger) in truth the exemplary experience of the two sons of Adam, when they each offered a sacrifice, and it was accepted from one of them, and not accepted
from the other. "I will surely kill you," said (he whose sacrifice
was not accepted). "Allah accepts only from the sincere and
truly pious," said the other. (5:27)

In all our religious acts, our intention must be to please Allah
Almighty, and do them just because Allah Almighty wants us to
do them. We cannot have another aim such as gaining fame, or being approved and acclaimed by others, or obtaining some worldly status, advantage, post and position, or wealth. The Qur'an declares:

But they were not enjoined anything other than that they
should worship Allah, sincere in faith in Him and practicing
the Religion purely for His sake, as people of pure faith; and
establish the Prayer in accordance with its conditions; and pay
the Prescribed Purifying Alms. And that is the upright, ever-
true Religion. (98:5)

It also declares:

And far removed from it (the Fire) will be he who keeps
farthest away from disobedience to Allah in greater reverence for Him and piety; who spends his wealth (in Allah's
cause and for the needy) so that he may grow in purity,
without anyone who has favored him so that he should
spend in return for it, nor expecting any reward in return
for what he spends. (Rather, he spends) only in longing for
the good pleasure of his Lord, the Most High. He will certainly be contented (he with his Lord and his Lord with
him). (92:17–21)

The Qur'an also reminds us that Satan cannot deceive Allah's
servants endowed with sincerity in faith and worship as follows:

(*Iblis* said:) "My Lord! Because You have allowed me to rebel and go astray, I will indeed deck out as appealing to them on the earth (the worldly, material dimension of human existence and the path of error), and I will surely cause them all to rebel and go astray, except Your servants from among them, endowed with sincerity in faith and Your worship." (Allah) said: "This (path of sincerity in faith) is a straight path that I have taken upon Myself (to lead to Me). "My servants—you shall have no authority over any of them, unless it be such as follow you being rebellious (against Me, as you are)." (15:39–42)

Islam severely condemns two-facedness. The Prophet, upon him be peace and blessings, said, "He who is two-faced in this world will have two tongues of fire on the Day of Resurrection."[1] He also warned, saying, "The worst people in the Sight of Allah on the Day of Resurrection will be the two-faced people who appear to some people with one face and to other people with another face."[2]

HONOR, MIGHT, AND GLORY LIE IN FOLLOWING THE QUR'AN

Believers must search for honor, might, and glory only in following the Qur'an or being good servants of Allah. For Allah declares in the Qur'an:

Indeed, it (the Qur'an) is a Reminder for you and for your people, in which lie your honor and happiness (in both worlds). And you (all people) will be questioned (about how it was understood and how lived). (43:44)

All honor, might, and glory belong to Allah and, by His leave and due to following Him, to His Messenger and the believers:

Whoever seeks might and glory should know that all might and glory is for Allah (so let him seek from Him alone). (35:10)

(The hypocrites are) those who take unbelievers for confidants, guardians and allies in preference to the believers: do they seek might and glory in being together with them? (If so, let them know that) might and glory belong altogether to Allah. (4:139)

They say: "For certain, if we return to Medina, those with more status and power will drive out from it the weaker and lowlier ones." But all glory and might belong to Allah, and (by His leave) to His Messenger and the believers. But (being incapable of knowledge of the truth) the hypocrites do not know this. (63:8)

Believers do not fear the censure of any who censure in following the Qur'an and striving in His cause. The Qur'an declares:

O you who believe! Whoever of you turns away from his Religion, (know that) in time, Allah will raise up a people whom He loves, and who love Him, most humble towards the believers, dignified and commanding in the face of the unbelievers, striving (continuously and in solidarity) in Allah's cause, and fearing not the censure of any who censure. That is Allah's grace and bounty, which He grants to whom He wills. Allah is All-Embracing (with His profound grace), All-Knowing. (5:54)

FOLLOWING KNOWLEDGE AND AVOIDING GROUNDLESS ASSERTIONS AND CONJECTURES

Islam attaches extreme importance to knowledge and orders us to avoid groundless assertions and conjectures, and follow knowledge:

Do not follow that of which you have no knowledge (whether it is good or bad), and refrain from groundless assertions and conjectures. Surely the hearing, the sight, and the heart—each of these is subject to questioning about it (you are answerable, and will be called to account, for each of these on the Day of Judgment). (17:36)

The hearing, the sight, and the heart are the three means of acquiring knowledge. We must follow whatever we hear undoubtedly or see undoubtedly, and we must be exactly certain of what we hear, see, and learn. We must particularly be careful about our beliefs and statements concerning Allah Almighty:

> And yet, among people there are some who dispute about Allah without having any true knowledge or any true guidance, or an enlightening (Divine) Book. They keep on disputing arrogantly to lead people astray from Allah's way. For such there is disgrace in the world, and on the Day of Resurrection, We will cause them to taste the punishment of the scorching Fire. (22:8-9)

> Do you not see that Allah has made all that is in the heavens and all that is on the earth of service to you, and lavished on you His favors, outward and inward? And yet, among people are those who dispute about Allah without having any true knowledge or any true guidance, or an enlightening (Divine) Book. (31:20)

The verses quoted cite three sources that one should base oneself on to have correct knowledge of Allah. These are: (i) knowledge obtained through the study of, and reflection on, the creation in the light of the Revelation, and through the disciplines of the spiritual way; and (ii) true guidance, by which it refers to the Divine Revelation or inspiration; and (iii) the Divine Book, which illuminates minds and hearts.

The Qur'an, which orders having exact knowledge in order to make a judgment about something, and forbids following conjecture and imitation which is not based on knowledge, warns that those who reckon that they are doing good without their self-estimation being based on certain knowledge are the greatest losers in respect of their deeds:

> When such people are told to follow what Allah has sent down, they say: "No, but we follow that (the traditions, customs, beliefs, and practices) which we found our forefathers in." What! Even if Satan is inviting them to the punishment of the Blaze (by suggesting to them the way of their forefathers)? (31:21)

> They (your false deities) are nothing but made-up names that you and your forefathers have invented; Allah sent no authori-

ty for them. They follow only conjecture and that which they themselves lust after. But now there has certainly come to them guidance from their Lord (Who has created them, and sustains them). (53:23)

Say: "Shall We inform you who are the greatest losers in respect of their deeds? Those whose endeavor has been wasted in this world (because it is directed only to this-worldly ends, and so it is bound to be wasted hereafter also) but who themselves reckon that they are doing good." (18:103–104)

The Qur'an also warns that conjecture can never substitute for anything of the truth (55:28). Insisting on following sure knowledge, the Qur'an orders us to verify any news based on unreliable sources:

O you who believe! If some transgressor brings you news (that requires taking action), verify it carefully (before you believe and act upon it), lest you harm a people in ignorance and then become regretful for what you have done. (49:6)

In addition to following accurate knowledge, refraining from conjectures and blind imitation, and verifying particularly any news we receive from unreliable sources, the Qur'an orders us to receive the necessary accurate information from or refer any news or unverified information to the people of expert knowledge:

We did not send before you (O Muhammad) any but men to whom We revealed—and if you (O people) do not know, then ask the people of expert knowledge (15:43).

Whenever any news comes to them, related to (public) security or alarm, they go about spreading it (without ascertaining if the news is true or not, and without thinking about whether it is beneficial or harmful to spread it). Whereas if they would but refer it to the Messenger and to those among them (in the community) who are entrusted with authority, those from among them who are competent to investigate it would bring to light what it is really about. (O believers!) Save for Allah's grace and mercy upon you, all but a few (of you) would have been (deceived by the hypocrites and) following Satan. (4:83)

REFRAINING FROM CUSTOMS OR TRADITIONS NOT IN COMPLIANCE WITH ISLAM

During their history, people form certain customs or traditions. Islam does not reject any customary or traditional practice approvable by it. Rather, it refers some of the people's social affairs to the customary good and religiously approvable practices among them. For example, although Islam itself has determined or established certain rights and duties between the husband and wife, such as the maintenance of the family on the part of the husband and guarding and keeping undisclosed what should be kept undisclosed concerning the family honor and her chastity on the part of the wife (4:34), it has referred some of those rights or duties such as the amount of the bridal-due, to customary good and religiously approvable practices established in the society (2:228; 4:25). However, Islam rejects the customary or traditional practices which do not comply with its essence and essential doctrines, and abolished those that were in force during its revelation. For example, there was a custom among the pagan Arabs that a husband would say to his wife, "You are henceforth as my mother's back to me," and thus removed himself from conjugal relations with his wife. This was the equivalent of an irrevocable divorce, but a woman thus divorced could not marry again. Islam abolished this custom (33:4; 58:2). Islam also abolished the practice of taking somebody into one's family as a relation, i.e., as a son or daughter, and declared that adoption has no legal effect (33:4). Therefore, we must refrain from the customs or traditions not in compliance with Islam.

REFRAINING FROM DISPUTE AND FORMING FACTIONS IN THE RELIGION

The Qur'an orders agreement, accord, and unity among Muslims. Preserving fellowship among Muslims is a certain sign or demonstration of sincerity in the Religion. The essentials of faith, worship, good morals, daily life, social relationships and economic interactions or business, and criminal law are so clear that everyone can understand and practice them. The only variations are related to secondary matters changeable according to time and circumstances. For this reason, it is extremely interesting that the Qur'an emphatically reiterates that the followers of the previous Scriptures differed and split into opposing factions because of envious rivalry and insolence among themselves only after the manifest truths and the knowledge (of the truth) had come to them (2:213; 3:19; 42:14).

It is quite natural that differences of opinion may arise among people concerning everyday affairs and secondary matters of the Religion. Islam forbids dispute and discussion without knowledge about all matters of the Religion and orders referring any matter or disagreement to those with expert knowledge:

> Do not follow that of which you have no knowledge (whether it is good or bad), and refrain from groundless assertions and conjectures. Surely the hearing, the sight, and the heart—each of these is subject to questioning about it (you are answerable, and will be called to account, for each of these on the Day of Judgment). (17:36)

> And yet, among people there are some who dispute about Allah without having any true knowledge or any true guidance, or an enlightening (Divine) Book. They keep on disputing arrogantly to lead people astray from Allah's way. For such there is disgrace in the world, and on the Day of Resurrection, We will cause them to taste the punishment of the scorching Fire. (22:8–9)

> Do you not see that Allah has made all that is in the heavens and all that is on the earth of service to you, and lavished on you His favors, outward and inward? And yet, among people are those who dispute about Allah without having any true knowledge or any true guidance, or an enlightening Divine Book. (31:20)

We did not send before you (O Muhammad) any but men to whom We revealed—and if you (O people) do not know, then ask the people of expert knowledge (15:43).

Whenever any news comes to them, related to (public) security or alarm, they go about spreading it (without ascertaining if the news is true or not, and without thinking about whether it is beneficial or harmful to spread it). Whereas if they would but refer it to the Messenger and to those among them (in the community) who are entrusted with authority, those from among them who are competent to investigate it would bring to light what it is really about. (O believers!) Save for Allah's grace and mercy upon, all but a few (of you) would have been (deceived by the hypocrites and) following Satan. (4:83)

Dispute and forming factions in the Religion is a cause of perdition in both worlds and Allah warns Muslims against it:

The Sabbath was ordained only for those who differed about it (not for all the communities that were to follow the way of Abraham). Your Lord will assuredly judge between them on the Day of Resurrection concerning that on which they used to differ. (16:124)

But people have broken up and differed among themselves as regards the Religion. But they are all bound to return to Us (to account for all that they did). Whoever does any deed of good and righteousness, being a true believer, his endeavor will not be left unrewarded in ingratitude. We are keeping the record of every good deed of his in his favor (without the least being neglected). (21:93–94)

Those who have made divisions in their Religion (whereas they must accept it in its totality), and have been divided into different parties—you have nothing to do with them. Their case rests with Allah, and then He will make them understand what they were doing. (6:159)

One of the ways to follow in order not to differ in the Religion and to preserve unity is refraining from asking much, and the Qur'an forbids it:

O you who believe! (Practice as you are admonished to practice, and) do not ask about things which, if made manifest to
you, would give you trouble (and make the practice of the
Religion difficult for you). Even so, if you ask about them
while the Qur'an is being sent down, they (what is necessary
to be made manifest) will be made manifest to you (to the
extent that Allah wills). (Many things that you have either
asked or want to ask about, but which Allah has left unspoken)
Allah has absolved you thereof: Allah is All-Forgiving, All-
Clement. Indeed a people before you used to ask such questions (and demanded from their Prophet such things as particular miracles) and, thereafter, they fell into unbelief (through
not carrying out the commandments given in answer to their
questions, or through willfully disbelieving in their Prophet,
despite the miracles worked). (5:101–102)

JUSTICE OR BALANCE, AND TRUE TESTIMONY, AND REFRAINING FROM GOING TO ANY EXTREMES

Justice is the basis of human individual and collective life. The word
used for both justice and balance in the terminology of the Qur'an
is *'adl*, meaning balance or establishing the balance or weighing and
measuring accurately.

The Qur'an mentions that Allah has set up the balance in the
creation and life of the universe, and calls us to observe the balance
with full equity in all of our dealings:

And the heaven—He has made it high (above the earth), and
He has set up the balance, so you must not go beyond (the
limits with respect to) the balance; and observe the balance
with full equity, and do not fall short in it. (55:7–9)

The Qur'an also mentions that Allah has sent down the Balance
together with the Book and iron so that humanity may live in equity:

Assuredly We have sent Our Messengers with manifest truths
(and clear proofs of their being Messengers), and We have sent
down with them the Book and the Balance so that (relations
among) humankind may live in equity. And We have sent
down iron, in which is stern might and benefits for human-

kind, so that Allah may mark out those who help (the cause
of) Allah and His Messengers, though they do not see Him.
Surely Allah is All-Strong, All-Glorious with irresistible might.
(57:25)

This verse is very significant especially in assessing a sound society and government. The Messengers are the God-appointed lead-
ers of humankind, who always guide humans to the truth and led
them in all aspects of life throughout human history. The Book is
the compilation of knowledge, instructions, and laws essential to
their happiness in both worlds. The Balance is the criterion to attain what is right in belief, thinking, and action, and also to realize
justice in human individual and social life. Besides being a very important mineral for human life, particularly for the development of
industry, iron also symbolizes force or power in human social life.
Without the Book, iron (force) destroys justice and brings about
injustice. Without the Balance, iron misuses the Book according to
its own benefits. Without iron, the Book and Balance are not sufficient to form a good society and government. Said Nursi remarks,
"Principles of wisdom and laws of truth have no effect upon ordinary people unless the former are combined with the state's laws
and the latter with power."[3]

The establishment of balance or the realization of justice in human individual and social life requires refraining from going into all
extremes. For example, the Qur'an declares:

> O you who believe! Do not hold as unlawful the pure, whole-
> some things that Allah has made lawful to you, and do not
> exceed the bounds (either by making forbidden what is lawful,
> or by over-indulgence in the lawful). Allah does not love those
> who exceed the bounds. (5:87)

> And (the true servants of the All-Merciful are those) who, when
> they spend (both for their own and others' needs), are neither
> wasteful nor niggardly, and (are aware that) there is a happy
> mean between those (two extremes). (25:67)

The Qur'an praises the Community of Muhammad as being a middle-way community:

> And in that way (O Community of Muhammad, whereas others turn in different directions and, straying from the Straight Path, falter between extremes in thought and belief), We have made you a middle-way community, that you may be witnesses for the people (as to the ways they follow), and that the (most noble) Messenger may be a witness for you. (2:143)

As mentioned before, justice is the establishment of the balance. The Qur'an decisively orders judging with equity and justice, without ever following the desires and caprices of people. It also warns that judging with justice and equity is possible by judging with what Allah has sent down:

> But if you judge, judge between them with equity and justice. Surely Allah loves the scrupulously equitable. (5:42)

> (Thus did We command you:) Judge between them with what Allah has sent down, and do not follow their desires and caprices, and beware of them lest they tempt you away from any part of what Allah has sent down to you. If they turn away, then know that Allah wills only to afflict them for some of their sins. And many among human beings are indeed transgressors. (5:49)

Bearing witnesses to the truth without concealing it and giving true testimony even though it is against our own selves or parents or kindred are among the basic means or requirements to establish justice:

> O you who believe! Be upholders and standard-bearers of justice, bearing witness to the truth for Allah's sake, even though it be against your own selves, or parents or kindred. Whether the person concerned be rich or poor, (bear in mind that) Allah is nearer to them (than you are and more concerned with their well-being). So do not (in expectation of some gain from the rich or out of misplaced compassion for the poor) follow your own desires lest you swerve from justice. If you distort

(the truth) or decline (to bear truthful witness), then know
that Allah is fully aware of all that you do. (4:135)

The Qur'an particularly warns that our love or detestation for a
people must not cause us to violate justice:

> And never let your detestation for a people, because they
> barred you from the Sacred Mosque, move you to commit
> violations (acts of aggression or injustice). (5:2)

> O you who believe! Be upholders and standard-bearers of right
> for Allah's sake, being witnesses for (the establishment of)
> absolute justice. And by no means let your detestation for a
> people (or their detestation for you) move you to (commit the
> sin of) deviating from justice. Be just: this is nearer and more
> suited to righteousness and piety. Seek righteousness and piety,
> and always act in reverence for Allah. Surely Allah is fully
> aware of all that you do. (5:8)

> (The witnesses shall swear by Allah, and say:) "We will not sell
> our testimony for any price, even if it concerns one near of
> kin, nor will we conceal the testimony of Allah (namely, the
> truth), for then we would surely be among the sinful."
> (5:106)

The following verse is one of the most comprehensive Qur'anic
statements concerning the rules of a happy life in both worlds:

> Allah enjoins justice (and right judgment in all matters), and
> devotion to doing good, and generosity towards relatives; and
> He forbids you indecency, wickedness, and vile conduct (all
> offenses against religion, life, personal property, chastity, and
> health of mind and body). He exhorts you (repeatedly) so that
> you may reflect and be mindful! (16:90)

Abu Bakr, may Allah be pleased with him, narrates:

> Allah's Messenger said three times, "Shall I not inform you of
> the biggest of the major sins?" We said, "Yes, O Allah's
> Messenger!" He said, "To join partners in worship with Allah:
> to be undutiful to one's parents." The Prophet sat up after he
> had been reclining and added, "And I warn you against giving

forged statement and a false witness; I warn you against giving a forged statement and a false witness." The Prophet kept on saying that warning till we thought that he would not stop.[4]

REFRAINING FROM HOLDING ONESELF PURE AND JUDGING OTHERS

Humanity is fallible by nature, and we commit many sins every day. Also, we cannot exactly know the true nature of our deeds and their consequences and how good or bad they are in Allah's sight. Neither can we know whether all of our deeds that we do because Islam orders them are accepted by Allah. Because of this, Islam forbids that we sanctify ourselves or hold ourselves pure; it always orders humility and modesty. The Qur'an says:

> Those who avoid the major sins and indecent, shameful deeds (which are, in fact, included in the major sins), only falling into small faults—surely your Lord is of extensive forgiveness. He knows you well when He originates you from (the particles of) earth, and when you are hidden (fetuses) in the wombs of your mothers. So do not hold yourselves pure (sinless; it is vain self-justification). He knows best him who keeps from disobedience to Allah in reverence for Him and piety. (53:32)

The Qur'an quotes Prophet Joseph, upon him be peace, who, although sinless as a Prophet, did not claim to be free of error, saying:

> "Yet I do not claim myself free of error, for assuredly the human carnal soul always commands evil, except that my Lord has mercy (which saves us from committing evil acts). Surely my Lord is All-Forgiving, All-Compassionate (especially toward His believing servants)." (12:53)

Islam, which forbids self-sanctification, also forbids judging others and seeing them as sinful and condemned to Hellfire. Abu Hurayra, may Allah be pleased with him, narrates:

> I heard Allah's Messenger, upon him be peace and blessings, say, "There were two men among the Children of Israel, who were striving for the same goal. One of them would commit sin

and the other would strive to do his best in the world. The man who exerted himself in worship continued to see the other in sin. He would say, "Refrain from it." One day he found him in sin and said to him, "Refrain from it." The other retorted, "Leave me alone with my Lord. Have you been sent as a watchman over me?" He said, "I swear by Allah, Allah will not forgive you, nor will He admit you to Paradise." Then their souls were taken back (by Allah), and they met together with the Lord of the worlds.

He (Allah) said to the man who had striven hard in worship, "Had you knowledge about Me or had you power over that which I had in My hand?" He said to the man who sinned, "Go and enter Paradise by My mercy." He said about the other, "Take him to Hell."

Abu Hurayra said, "By Him in Whose hand my soul is, he spoke a word by which this world and the next world of his were destroyed."[5]

The Prophet, upon him be peace and blessings, said, "When a person says that people are ruined, he is himself ruined."[6]

The Qur'an orders us to consider how we are faring along our own way without busying ourselves with those who follow different ways. It says as follows:

> O you who believe! (Do not busy yourselves with those who follow different ways!) Your responsibility is your selves (so consider how you are faring along your own way). Those who go astray can do you no harm if you yourselves are guided (and so know the right way, and then follow it without deviation). To Allah is the return of all of you, and He will make you understand all that you were doing (and call you to account for it). (5:105)

ASKING FOR FORGIVENESS FOR ONE'S FAULTS AND THANKFULNESS

We are fallible beings; besides, we are absolutely unable to give the necessary thanks to Allah for His favors. Therefore, we always need to ask for His forgiveness. Although he was sinless, Allah's Messenger, upon him be peace and blessings, asked for Allah's forgiveness more than seventy times a day.[7] Even he would say, "There is (at times) some sort of shade upon my heart, and I seek forgiveness from Allah a hundred times a day."[8]

Allah Almighty declares in the Qur'an that He will not destroy a Muslim people so long they continue to seek forgiveness from Him (8:33). It shows sufficiently the importance of seeking forgiveness from Allah that the Almighty orders us to ask for His forgiveness not only for the sins we have committed but also after any achievement He has favored us with. For example:

> When Allah's help comes, and victory (which is a door to further victories), and you see people entering Allah's Religion in throngs, then glorify your Lord with His praise, and ask Him for forgiveness; for He surely is One Who returns repentance with liberal forgiveness and additional reward. (110:1–3)

The order to glorify Allah with His praise and to ask Him for forgiveness is a warning to the believers that they should never fall into the perilous error of attributing victory to themselves, and that they should always be careful to avoid indulging in sins after a victory. The victory is not their achievement; rather, it is Allah Who bestows victory on His servants. Moreover, we can put up with hardships and persecutions, but it is more difficult to be firm and unyielding against the temptations of the carnal soul, particularly in times of ease that come after years of privation and persecution.

Our achievements in Allah's cause are in fact the reason for our forgiveness. The Qur'an declares:

> We have surely granted you a manifest victory (which is a door to further victories), that Allah may forgive you (O Messenger) your lapses of the past and those to follow, and complete His favor on you, and guide you (to steadfastness) on a straight path (leading to Allah's being pleased with You and eternal happiness); And that Allah may help you to a glorious, mighty achievement. (48:1–3)

Allah loves our seeking forgiveness from Him just after committing a sin without any delay, and wants His servants to do so.

> ....Allah loves (such) people who are devoted to doing good, aware that Allah is seeing them. They are also the ones who, when they have committed a shameful deed or wronged themselves (through any kind of sinful act), immediately remember Allah and implore Him to forgive their sins—for who will forgive sins save Allah?—and do not persist knowingly in whatever (evil) they have committed. Such are the ones whose reward is forgiveness from their Lord and Gardens through which rivers flow, to abide therein. How excellent is the reward of those who always do good deeds! (3:134–136)

It is highly significant that however much reward we have earned, we cannot enter Paradise without Allah's forgiveness:

> And hasten, as if competing with one another, to forgiveness from your Lord, and to a Garden as spacious as the heavens and the earth, prepared for the God-revering, pious. (3:133)

> Such are the ones whose reward is forgiveness from their Lord and Gardens through which rivers flow, to abide therein. How excellent is the reward of those who always do good deeds! (3:136)

The Qur'an relates that the believers will ask Allah for forgiveness before they enter Paradise, as follows:

> O you who believe! Turn to Allah in sincere and reforming repentance. It is hoped that your Lord will blot your evil deeds from you and admit you into Gardens through which rivers flow, on a Day when Allah will not disgrace nor disappoint the Prophet and those who believe in his company. Their (the believers') light will shine and spread before them, and on their right hands, as they say: "Our Lord! Perfect our light (by Your grace, so that we may reach Paradise), and forgive us. Surely You have full power over everything!" (66:8)

The Qur'an usually mentions Allah's forgiveness together or before Paradise or its bounties (2:221; 5:9; 8:4, 74; 11:11; 22:50; and so on).

It can be said that true humanity lies in two important virtues, which may serve as the means of a person's guidance. One of them is that people acknowledges their innate weakness and poverty, and the errors they have committed, and pray for forgiveness. The other is that they feel gratitude for Allah's favors. The Qur'an declares:

> And (remember also) when your Lord proclaimed: "If you are thankful (for My favors), I will most certainly give you more; but if you are ungrateful, surely My punishment is severe." (14:7)

> Indeed, your Lord is gracious and bountiful for humankind, but most of them do not give thanks. (27:73)

> We surely granted wisdom to Luqman, and said: "Give thanks to Allah." Whoever gives thanks to Allah, gives thanks but for (the good of) his own soul; and whoever is ungrateful, surely Allah is the All-Wealthy and Self-Sufficient (absolutely independent of the whole creation), All-Praiseworthy. (31:12)

Asking Allah for forgiveness and thanking Him lead us to be able also to apologize to people for any evil we may have done to them or thank them for any good we receive through their hands. The Prophet, upon him be peace and blessings, said, "He who does not thank Allah does not thank people."[9]

Haughtiness and ingratitude are usually reasons for unbelief. One who never feels remorse or asks forgiveness for their errors and is unaware of gratitude or being thankful cannot be regarded as being truly human. A person whose conscience has not been fully darkened does not refrain from acknowledging their errors, and is appreciative of any good they receive. This is why the Qur'an, on the one hand, reminds people of Allah's favors upon them, thereby arousing in them a feeling of gratitude and thankfulness, while on the other hand, it calls on them to acknowledge their errors and sins and to ask for forgiveness. This is very important, both in being truly human and in making people accept Divine truths and guidance.

Concerning thankfulness, Fethullah Gülen writes as follows:

Thankfulness is to be reflected in the person's actions or daily life, in speech and in the heart.

> One may thank Allah verbally by only depending upon His Power and Might, as well as upon His bestowal or withholding of favors, and acknowledging that all good and bounties come from Him. Verbal thankfulness also means daily recitation of portions of the Qur'an, prayers, supplications, and Allah's Names. As He alone creates all good, beauty, and bounty, as well as the means by which they can be obtained, only He sends them at the appropriate time. Since He alone determines, apportions, creates, and spreads [all our provisions] before us as "heavenly tables," He alone deserves our gratitude and thanks. Attributing our attainment of His bounties to our own or to another's means or causes, in effect thereby proclaiming that He is not the true Owner, Creator, and Giver of all bounty, is like giving a huge tip to the servant who lays before us a magnificent table and ignoring the host who is responsible for having it prepared and sent to us. Such an attitude reflects sheer ignorance and ingratitude, as mentioned in, *They only know (what reaches to their senses from) the outward aspect of the life of this world, but they are heedless and unaware of (what lies beyond it and) the Hereafter* (30:7).
>
> Thankfulness by the heart means that one is certain or convinced of the truth of the Islamic faith and straightforwardness. It also means that, as mentioned above, whatever good and whatever favor we have, it is from Allah and by His bestowing. Practical or bodily thankfulness means using one's organs, faculties, and abilities for the purposes for which they were created, and performing the duties of servanthood falling on each. Since thankfulness relates directly to all aspects or branches of belief and worship, it is regarded as half of the faith. With respect to this inclusiveness, it is considered together with patience, meaning that according to some people, thankfulness and patience are considered as the two halves of religious life.[10]

PATIENCE

Patience means endurance or bearing pains, sufferings and difficulties and showing resistance against them and dealing with problems calmly. Because of its importance, patience is regarded as half of the religious life, the other half of which is thankfulness.

The Qur'an either orders patience itself in its many verses such as, *Seek help through patience and through the Prayer* (2:45); and, *O you who believe! Be patient; encourage each other to patience, vying in it with one another and outdoing all others in it; and observe your duties to Allah in solidarity, and keep from disobedience to Allah in due reverence for Him and piety, so that you may prosper (in both worlds); and be patient, persevering (in doing good, avoiding mistakes, and against all kinds of persecution you are made to suffer in Allah's cause), for surely Allah never leaves to waste the reward of those devoted to doing good, aware that Allah is seeing them* (11:115); or the Qur'an prohibits acts opposed to patience in verses such as, *Show not haste concerning them (the unbelievers)!* (46:35); and, *When you meet in battle those who disbelieve, turn not your backs to them* (8:15). In many verses of the Qur'an, Allah praises the patient or declares that He loves them or mentions the ranks He has bestowed on them. For example, *The patient and steadfast, and the truthful and loyal...* (3:17); *Allah loves the patient* (3:146); and *Surely, Allah is with the patient* (2:153).

The following verses are especially important for patience:

> (So O believers, as a requirement of the wisdom in, and purpose for, your life of the world,) you will surely be tested in respect of your properties and your selves, and you will certainly hear many hurtful things from those who were given the Book before you and those who associate partners with Allah. If you remain patient (are steadfast in your Religion, and observe the bounds set by Allah in your relations with them) and keep within the limits of piety (in obeying Allah, and in your conduct toward them), (know that) this is among meritorious things requiring great resolution to fulfill. (2:186)

O you who believe! Seek help (against all kinds of hardships and tribulations) through patience and the Prayer; surely Allah is with the patient. And say not of those who are killed in Allah's cause, "They are dead." Rather they are alive, but you are not aware. We will certainly test you with something of fear and hunger, and loss of wealth and lives and fruits (earnings); but give glad tidings to the patient: those who, when a disaster befalls them, say, "Surely we belong to Allah (as His creatures and servants), and surely to Him we are bound to return." (And they act accordingly.) Such are those upon whom are blessings from their Lord (such as forgiveness, answering their calls and satisfying their needs) and mercy (to come in the form of help in both this world and Hereafter, and favors in Paradise beyond human imagination); and they are the rightly guided ones. (2:153–157)

The Qur'an mentions patience from many other viewpoints or with respect to its many other aspects. For example, in the verses, *If you endure patiently, this is indeed better for those who are patient. Endure patiently; your endurance is only for Allah's sake and by His help; and do not grieve for them (because of their attitude toward your mission), nor be distressed because of what they scheme"* (16:126–127), it advises patience as a preferable way in relations with unbelievers while communicating Allah's Message to them. In the verse, *We will certainly bestow on those who are patient their reward according to the best of what they used to do* (16:96), it consoles the patient with the best rewards to be given in the Hereafter. In the verse, *If you have patience, and guard yourselves against evil and disobedience, Allah will send to your aid five thousand angels having distinguishing marks, if they suddenly attack you* (3:125), it promises the believers Divine aid in return for patience.

The Prophet, upon him be peace and blessings, said, "How remarkable a believer's affair is! For it is always to his advantage, and this is peculiar to none other than a believer. If something good happens to him, he gives thanks to Allah and this is to his advantage, and if something harmful happens to him, he endures it, and this is to his advantage also."[11] He also said, "None is more patient than Allah against the harmful saying. He hears from the people they ascribe children to Him, yet He gives them health and (supplies them with) provision."[12]

With respect to the things requiring patience, patience can be divided into the following categories:

- Enduring the difficulties of fulfilling the duty of servanthood to Allah or steadfastness in performing regular, periodical acts of worship;
- showing resistance to the temptations of the evil-commanding carnal soul and Satan to commit sins;
- enduring heavenly or earthly calamities, which includes resignation to Divine decrees;
- steadfastness in following the right path without any deviations in the face of worldly attractions;
- showing no haste in realizing one's hopes or plans which require a certain length of time to achieve.

The Prophet, upon him be peace and blessings, was once dividing and distributing war-gains. A man said, "By Allah, the pleasure of Allah has not been intended in this division." That was hard upon the Prophet, upon him be peace and blessings, and the color of his face changed. Then, he said, "Moses was harmed with more than this, yet he remained patient."[13]

> And be patient, persevering (in doing good, avoiding mistakes, and against all kinds of persecution you are made to suffer in Allah's cause), for surely Allah never leaves to waste the reward of those devoted to doing good, aware that Allah is seeing them. (11:115)

DOING SOMETHING WITH EXCELLENCE AND KEEPING PURE AND CLEAN

We discussed in the second volume of this series what great importance Islam attaches to cleanliness and purity. The Qur'an, which orders us to keep away from all pollution (74:4–5), encourages us to immediately repent and ask for Allah's forgiveness for any sin with which we have polluted our hearts, and praises the believers who do so. For example:

> They are also the ones who, when they have committed a shameful deed or wronged themselves (through any kind of sinful act), immediately remember Allah and implore Him to forgive their sins—for who will forgive sins save Allah?—and do not persist knowingly in whatever (evil) they have committed. (3:135)

> ....if any of you does a bad deed due to ignorance (an instance of defeat to the evil-commanding soul), and thereafter repents and mends his way and conduct, surely He is All-Forgiving, All-Compassionate." (6:54)

> Those who keep from disobedience to Allah in reverence for Him and piety: when a suggestion from Satan touches them—they are alert and remember Allah, and then they have clear discernment. (7:201)

Islam, which wants us to keep pure and clean and be immediately purified of any dirt, also orders us to do with excellence whatever we do. The Qur'an frequently calls us to believe and do good, righteous, and sound deeds (2:25, 62, 82, 277; 3:57; 4:57, 122, 173, and so on), and Allah's Messenger, upon him be peace and blessings, says that Allah likes His servants do with excellence whatever they do. The Messenger also says, "Allah is the All-Beautiful and likes what is beautiful, the All-Pure and likes what is clean and pure, the All-Bestower and likes those who bestow, and the All-Generous and likes those who are generous. Therefore, keep your houseyards clean as you keep your houses clean."[14]

The Qur'an warns us that we are under inspection in all our deeds and will be called to account for them, saying:

> Say: "Work, and Allah will see your work, and so will His Messenger and the true believers; and you will be brought back to the Knower of the Unseen and the witnessed, and He will make you understand all that you were doing (and call you to account for it)." (9:105)

IHSAN OR PERFECT GOODNESS

Ihsan has two literal meanings, doing something well and perfectly and doing someone a favor, and is used in the Qur'an and the Sunna with either meaning or to encompass both meanings.

Ihsan or perfect goodness is an action of the heart that involves thinking according to the standards of truth; forming the intention to do good, useful things and then doing them; and performing acts of worship in the consciousness that Allah sees them. To attain perfect goodness, believers must establish their thoughts, feelings, and conceptions on firm belief, and then deepen that belief by practicing the essentials of Islam and training their heart to receive Divine gifts and illuminating it with the His Light. One who has attained such a degree of perfect goodness can really do good to others just for Allah's sake, without expecting any return. According to a Prophetic saying, "Perfect goodness is that you worship Allah as if seeing Him; for even if you do not see Him, He certainly sees you."[15] The most comprehensive and precise meaning of perfect goodness is that there is no fault in believers' actions, and that they are always conscious of Allah's oversight. Doing good to others is an essential attribute of their nature. *Ihsan*, in the sense of doing good to others, is summed up in the Prophetic principle of desiring for one's fellow Muslim whatever one desires for oneself.[16] Its universal dimension is defined in the Prophetic Tradition, "Surely, Allah has decreed that you excel in whatever you do. When you punish someone by killing, do it kindly; when you slaughter an animal, slaughter it kindly. Let him who will slaughter it sharpen his knife and avoid giving the animal much pain."[17] In many of its verses, the Qur'an encourages perfect goodness and praises the believers who have attained it. For example:

> And be patient, persevering (in doing good, avoiding mistakes, and against all kinds of persecution you are made to suffer in Allah's cause), for surely Allah never leaves to waste the reward of those devoted to doing good, aware that Allah is seeing them. (11:115)

When Joseph reached his full manhood, We granted him authority with sound, wise judgment, and special knowledge. Thus, do We reward those devoted to doing good as if seeing Allah. (12:22)

As for the God-revering, pious: they will be in Gardens and springs, Taking whatever their Lord grants them. For they were, before that, devoted to doing Allah's commands, aware that Allah was seeing them. (51:15–16)

HUMILITY AND REFRAINING FROM EXULTATION AND CONCEIT OR HAUGHTINESS

Islam never approves of exultation and conceit and haughtiness. Instead, it orders sobriety, humility and modesty, and being and behaving as one from among the ordinary people. The Qur'an declares:

Do not turn your face from people in scornful pride, nor move on the earth haughtily. Surely Allah does not love anyone proud and boastful. Be modest in your bearing, and subdue your voice. For certain, the most repugnant of voices is the braying of donkeys." (31:18–19)

Do not strut about the earth in haughty self-conceit; for you can never split the earth (no matter how hard you stamp your foot), nor can you stretch to the mountains in height (no matter how strenuously you seek to impress). The evil of all this is abhorrent in the sight of your Lord. (17:37–38)

Do not exult in your wealth; surely Allah does not love those who exult. (28:76)

That (His leading you astray and your punishment) is because you arrogantly exulted on the earth without (sense of the bounds of) right, and because you were arbitrary in your exulting. Now enter through the gates of Hell to abide therein. How evil, indeed, is the dwelling of those (too) haughty (to acknowledge the truth)! (40:75–76)

Fethullah Gülen writes about modesty and humility (*tawadu*) as follows:

> *Tawadu* (modesty and humility) is the opposite of arrogance, pride, and haughtiness. It can also be interpreted as one's awareness of one's real position before Allah, and as letting that realization guide one's conduct toward Allah and with people. If one sees oneself as an ordinary, individual part of creation, a threshold of a door, a mat spread on a floor or a pavement stone, a pebble in a stream or chaff in a field, and if one can sincerely confess, as did Muhammad Lutfi Effendi, "Everybody else is good but I am bad; everybody else is wheat but I am chaff," the inhabitants of the heavens will kiss him or her on the head. In a narration attributed to the truthful, confirmed one, upon him be peace and blessings, it is said, "Charity does not in any way decrease the wealth; the servant who forgives, Allah adds to his respect, and the one who shows humility, Allah elevates him in the estimation (of the people)."[18] Thus, one's true greatness is inversely proportional to behaving as if one were great, just as one's true smallness is inversely proportional to behaving as if one were small. Humility has been defined in many ways: seeing oneself as devoid of all virtues essentially originating in oneself, treating others humbly and respectfully, seeing oneself as the worst of humanity (unless being honored by a special Divine treatment), and being alert to any stirring of the ego and immediately suppressing it. Each definition expresses a dimension of humility.
>
> Concerning humility, the glory of humanity, upon him be peace and blessings, declared, "Allah has revealed to me that you must be humble, and that no one must oppress another and must boast over another"[19]; and, "Shall I inform you about the people of Paradise? They comprise obscure unimportant humble people, and if one (among them) swears by Allah's Name that he will do that thing, Allah will fulfill his oath (by doing that). Shall I inform you about the people of the Fire? They comprise every cruel, violent, proud and conceited person"[20]; and, "Allah exalts one who is humble. That one sees himself as small while he is truly great in the sight of people."[21]

The glory of humanity, upon him be peace and blessings, lived as the most humble of people. He stopped at the places where children were gathered and played with and greeted them.[22] If someone held him by the hand and wanted to lead him somewhere, he never objected. (Anas ibn Malik said, "Any of the female slaves of Medina could take hold of the hand of Allah's Messenger, upon him be peace and blessings, and take him wherever she wished."[23]) He helped his wives with the housework.[24] When people were working, he worked with them.[25] He mended his shoes and clothes, milked sheep, and fed animals.[26] He sat at the table with his servant.[27] He always welcomed the poor warmly, looked after widows and orphans,[28] visited the ill, followed funeral processions, and answered the call of slaves in his community.[29] All beloved servants of Allah, those honored with nearness to Allah, have held that the signs of greatness in the great are humility and modesty, while the signs of smallness in the small are arrogance and vanity. Based on this understanding, they sought to show men and women how to become perfect.[30]

Conceit or haughtiness is among the basic reasons of unbelief and associating partners with Allah:

> I will turn away from My Revelations and signs those who act with haughtiness on the earth against all right. And though they see every sign, they do not believe in it; and though they see the way of right guidance, they do not take it as a way to follow. But if they see the way of error and rebellion against the truth, they take it as a way to follow. That is because they deny Our Revelations and are ever heedless of them. (7:146)

Allah's Messenger, upon him be peace and blessings, warned, "Allah, the All-Exalted and Glorious, said, 'Glory is My lower garment and Majesty is My cloak and whoever contends with Me in regard to them I will torment him.'"[31]

Allah's Messenger, upon him be peace and blessings, was the most humble and modest of people. He never liked being praised and addressed with any title of greatness. 'Abdullah ibn al-Shikhkhir, may Allah be pleased with him, narrates:

> I went with a deputation of Banu Amir to Allah's Messenger,
> upon him be peace and blessings, and we said, "You are our
> lord (*sayyid*)." To this he replied, "The Lord is Allah, the
> Blessed and Exalted." Then we said, "And the one of us most
> endowed with excellence and superiority." To this he replied,
> "Say what you have to say, or part of what you have to say,
> and do not let the devil make you his agent."[32]

Overcoming Anger

One of the basic faculties or powers with which Allah Almighty has
equipped humankind is anger. He has given it to humankind as the
source of their defense mechanism. If humankind can use it in the
right way, it becomes the origin of courage and forbearance, but if
humankind is overpowered or defeated by it, then it becomes fu-
ry and rashness, and can lead its owner to perdition or committing
great excesses. For this reason, we must discipline or purify and
train our power of anger. The Qur'an praises those who restrain
their rage and pardon people:

> And hasten, as if competing with one another, to forgiveness
> from your Lord, and to a Garden as spacious as the heavens
> and the earth, prepared for the God-revering, pious. They
> spend (out of what Allah has provided for them,) both in ease
> and hardship, ever-restraining their rage (even when provoked
> and able to retaliate), and pardoning people (their offenses).
> Allah loves (such) people who are devoted to doing good,
> aware that Allah is seeing them. They are also the ones who,
> when they have committed a shameful deed or wronged them-
> selves (through any kind of sinful act), immediately remember
> Allah and implore Him to forgive their sins – for who will for-
> give sins save Allah?—and do not persist knowingly in what-
> ever (evil) they have committed. Such are the ones whose
> reward is forgiveness from their Lord and Gardens through
> which rivers flow, to abide therein. How excellent is the
> reward of those who always do good deeds! (3:133–134)

Allah's Messenger, upon him be peace and blessings, said, "If anyone suppresses anger when he is in a position to give vent to it, Allah

will fill his heart with security and faith."[33] He also said, "The strong is not the one who overcomes the people by his strength (or wrestles well), but the strong is the one who controls himself while in anger."[34]

A man said to the Prophet, upon him be peace and blessings, "Advise me!" The Prophet, upon him be peace and blessings, said, "Do not become angry and furious." The man asked (the same) again and again, and the Prophet, upon him be peace and blessings, said in each case, "Do not become angry and furious."[35]

Abu Dharr, may Allah be pleased with him, narrates:

> Allah's Messenger, upon him be peace and blessings, said to us, "When one of you becomes angry while standing, he should sit down. If the anger leaves him, well and good; otherwise he should lie down."[36]

The Messenger also advises, "Anger comes from the devil, the devil was created of fire, and fire is extinguished only with water; so when one of you becomes angry, he should perform ablution."[37]

The Prophet, upon him be peace and blessings, also said, "I guarantee a house in the surroundings of Paradise for a man who avoids quarrelling even if he were in the right, a house in the middle of Paradise for a man who avoids lying even if he were joking, and a house in the upper part of Paradise for a man who made his character good."[38]

PROMOTING WHAT IS RIGHT AND GOOD AND FORBIDDING AND TRYING TO PREVENT EVIL

Promoting what is right and good and forbidding and trying to prevent evil is vital for the preservation of Islam and a Muslim community. The Qur'an explains that the basic purpose for the existence of the Muslim Community is doing this vital duty. It says:

> (O Community of Muhammad!) You are the best community ever brought forth for (the good of) humankind, enjoining and promoting what is right and good, and forbidding and

trying to prevent evil, and (this you do because) you believe in
Allah. (3:110)

Promoting what is right and good and forbidding and trying to
prevent evil is in fact the religious and social duty of every Muslim.
What follows is among the pieces of Luqman's advice to his son:

> "My dear son! Establish the Prayer in conformity with its con-
> ditions, enjoin and promote what is right and good, and for-
> bid and try to prevent evil, and bear patiently whatever may
> befall you. Surely (all of) that is among greatly meritorious
> things requiring great resolution to fulfill." (31:17)

It is not enough for the fulfillment of the duty of promoting what
is right and good and forbidding and trying to prevent evil that individuals perform it among themselves. Just as the Muslim Community
is the best community ever brought forth for the good of humankind
because they promote what is good and right and forbid and try to
prevent evil, there must also be a group or community which will do
this important duty in a systematic way. The Qur'an orders:

> There must be among you a community calling to good, and
> enjoining and actively promoting what is right, and forbidding
> and trying to prevent evil (in appropriate ways). They are
> those who are the prosperous. (3:104)

The Qur'an relates to us the tragic end of a people from among
the Children of Israel who would violate the Sabbath but were not
effectively prevented from doing so:

> Ask them about the township that was by the sea: how its peo-
> ple were violating the Sabbath when their fish came swimming
> to them on the day of their Sabbath, but on the day they did
> not keep Sabbath, they did not come to them. Thus did We test
> them as they were transgressing (all bounds). And when a com-
> munity of people among them asked (others who tried to
> restrain the Sabbath-breakers): "Why do you preach to a people
> whom Allah will destroy or punish with a severe punishment?"
> They said: "So as to have an excuse before your Lord, and so
> that they might keep from such disobedience in reverence for

Allah." Then, when they became heedless of all that they had been reminded of, We saved those who had tried to prevent the evil-doing, and seized the others who had been doing wrong with an evil punishment for their transgressions. Then, when they disdainfully persisted in doing what they had been forbidden to do, We said to them: "Be apes, miserably slinking and rejected!" (7:163–166)

REFRAINING FROM WHATEVER IS VAIN AND FRIVOLOUS

Humanity is, by nature, prone to play and sport, and spending time in a leisurely fashion. However, time is the greatest capital of humanity accorded to it to earn eternal happiness in the other world. Therefore, we must use time very carefully and not waste our life on frivolous things. While praising believers for their primary virtues at the beginning of *Surat al-Mu'minun* (23), the Qur'an mentions their turning away from whatever is vain and frivolous in the second rank, saying:

> Prosperous indeed are the believers. They are in their Prayer humble and fully submissive (being overwhelmed by the awe and majesty of Allah). They always turn away from and avoid whatever is vain and frivolous. (23:1–3)

Only those who have no sound belief in Allah and the other, eternal life, and do not pursue lofty ideals pursue worldly pleasures and are lost in vanities:

> They enjoyed their lot (in the world) for a while, and you have been enjoying your lot, just as those who preceded you enjoyed their lot; and you have plunged in self-indulgence, as others who plunged. Such (hypocrites and unbelievers) are those whose works have been wasted in both this world and the Hereafter, and those—they are the losers. (9:68–69)

> Yet (they do not desire certainty; instead) they are in an irrecoverable doubt, lost in the playthings of the worldly life. (44:9)

> Woe, then, on that Day to those who deny (Allah's Message and the Messengers)—Those who are habitually playing,

absorbed (in vanities): on that Day, they will be forcefully
thrust into the fire of Hell. (52:11–13)

However, Allah Almighty has not created the universe and humanity for fun and amusement. He has created them for universal,
meaningful purposes and on solid foundations of truth. So what is
expected of humans is to pursue these purposes and spend their life
following the truth. So, believers or true servants of Allah do not
take part in, nor bear witness to, any vanity or falsehood. Allah declares in the Qur'an:

> We have not created the heavens and the earth and all that is
> between them in play and fun. We have created them only
> with truth (for meaningful purposes, and on solid foundations
> of truth), but most people do not know. (44:38–39)

> And (those true servants of the All-Merciful are they) who do
> not take part in, or bear witness to, any vanity or falsehood
> (and who will not deem anything true unless they know it to
> be so for certain), and when they happen to pass by anything
> vain and useless, pass by it with dignity. (25:72)

Allah's Messenger, upon him be peace and blessings, said,
"Anybody who believes in Allah and the Last Day should not harm
his neighbor, and anybody who believes in Allah and the Last Day
should entertain his guest generously and anybody who believes in
Allah and the Last Day should say what is good or keep quiet."[39]

He also said, "It is owing to the beauty of the Muslimness of a
person that he abandons what is of no use to him."[40]

Being Merciful and Tender-Hearted

In the *Basmala*, the sacred formula of Islam, Allah Almighty presents Himself to us as being the All-Merciful, the All-Compassionate. M. Fethullah Gülen writes about compassion as follows:

> Compassion is the beginning of being; without it everything is
> chaos. Everything has come into existence through compassion
> and by compassion it continues to exist in harmony. The earth

was put in order by messages coming from the other side of the heavens. Everything from the macrocosm to the microcosm has achieved an extraordinary harmony thanks to compassion. The whole universe, in every particle of its being, ceaselessly sings the praises of the All-Compassionate. All creatures together extol compassion with voices peculiar to each. Humanity has a responsibility to show compassion to all living beings as a requirement of being human. The more they display compassion, the more exalted they become, while the more they resort to wrongdoing, oppression and cruelty, the more they are disgraced and humiliated.[41]

The Qur'an openly declares that Allah sent His Messenger, Muhammad, upon him be peace and blessings, but as an unequalled mercy for all the worlds (21:107). It praises Prophet Abraham, upon him be peace, for being most clement, tender-hearted, ever-turning to Allah with all his heart (11:75). This means that Islam, Allah's Religion revealed to humans for their happiness in both worlds, is purely a mercy for humankind. Allah's Messenger, whose mercy for all creation we will explain later, said concerning mercy or compassion, "Allah divided mercy into one hundred parts and He kept its ninety-nine parts with Him and sent down its one part on the earth, and because of that one single part, His creations are merciful to each other, so that even the mare lifts up her hoofs away from her foal, lest she should trample on it."[42] He also said, "He who is not merciful to others is not treated mercifully."[43] What follows are also among his sayings concerning being merciful or compassionate:

> The All-Merciful One has mercy on those who are merciful. If you show mercy to those who are on the earth, He Who is in the heaven (Who is above everything) will show mercy to you."[44]

The Prophet, upon him be peace and blessings, said, "Those who do not show mercy to our young ones and do not recognize the right of our elders are not from us."[45]

The Qur'an likens having hardened hearts to being like rocks, and severely criticizes hard-heartedness as follows:

> Then, a while after that, your hearts became hardened; they
> were like rocks, or even harder, for there are rocks from which
> rivers come gushing; there are some that split and water issues
> from them; and there are still others that roll down for fear
> and awe of Allah. (Whereas your hearts are harder than rocks,
> and) Allah is not unaware and unmindful of what you do.
> (2:74)

Out of his deep compassion, Allah's Messenger, upon him
be peace and blessings, kissed children and carried them on their
shoulders. For example, once he kissed Hasan ibn 'Ali, his beloved
grandson, while al-Aqra' ibn Habis at-Tamimi was sitting beside
him. Al-Aqra' said, "I have ten children and I have never kissed any
one of them." Allah's Messenger cast a look at him and said, "One
who is not merciful to others is not treated mercifully."[46] He also
said, "What can I do for you if Allah has removed mercy from your
heart?"[47]

RESPECTING ELDERS AND SHOWING COMPASSION FOR THE YOUNG

Islam stresses the importance of mutual respect and compassion
among people. We must especially be respectful to elders, scholars, and other people of similar standing, and show compassion for
the young. The Prophet said, "Those who do not respect elders and
show compassion for youths are not with us."[48]

We should be careful about our behavior in the company of
those whom we should respect, not raise our voices in their presence or call them as those of the same age and status call each other, and should refrain from affronting them. The teachings of the
Qur'an concerning how we must treat the Prophet, upon him be
peace and blessings, can shed light on the matter:

> O you who believe! Do not be forward in the Presence of
> Allah and His Messenger. Keep from disobedience to Allah in
> piety and reverence for Him, so that you may deserve His pro-
> tection. Surely Allah is All-Hearing, All-Knowing. O you who

believe! Do not raise your voices above the voice of the Prophet, nor speak loudly when addressing him, as you would speak loudly to one another, lest your good deeds go in vain without your perceiving it. (49:1–2)

Do not treat the Messenger's summoning and praying for you as your summoning and praying for one another. (24:63)

Those who affront Allah and His Messenger (through disrespect for Him in words and acts and for His Messenger and Islamic values), Allah certainly curses them (excludes them from His mercy) in this world and the Hereafter, and He has prepared for them a shameful, humiliating punishment. (33:57)

'Abdullah ibn 'Umar, may Allah be pleased with him, narrates that they (the Companions) kissed the hand of the Prophet, upon him be peace and blessings.[49] For example, when they returned from a military campaign, they kissed his hand.[50] It is acceptable, even recommended, to kiss the hands of one's parents and Muslim scholars, out of respect and piety, but unacceptable to kiss someone's hand for worldly reasons. It is also unacceptable to engage in flattery and sycophancy, bowing and bending before others.

Children usually kiss the hands of all their elders; after puberty, young people should kiss the hands of their mothers, fathers, grandparents, aunts and uncles, older siblings and parents-in-law. There is some disagreement regarding sons-in-law kissing the hands of mothers-in-law and daughters-in-law kissing the hands of fathers-in-law. There is no harm in kissing the hands of women advanced in age.

What has already been explained concerning mercifulness and tender-heartedness above may be enough to show how mercifully we treat the young.

ISLAM'S UNIVERSAL MERCY FOR ANIMALS

Islam's universal mercy embraces not only human beings, whether believers, People of the Book, or non-Muslims, but all other living creatures. First of all, the Qur'an presents animals forming communities like the communities of humanity:

> No living creature is there moving on the earth, no bird flying on its two wings, but they are communities like you. (6:38)

The Qur'an, which calls some of its chapters (The Cow/2, The Bee/16, The Ant/27, and The Spider/29) by the names of some animal species, mentions the bee as the animal endowed with special inspiration of Allah, and the ant as the animal able to understand human speech:

> And your Lord inspired the (female) bee: "Take for yourself dwelling-places in the mountains, and in the trees, and in what they (human beings) may build and weave. Then eat of all the fruits, and returning with your loads, follow the ways your Lord has made easy for you." There comes forth from their bellies a fluid of varying color, wherein is health for human beings. Surely, in this, there is a sign for people who reflect. (16:68–69)

> One day his hosts of jinn, and of men, and of birds were assembled before Solomon (upon his command), and were led forth under full control, until, when they reached a valley of ants, one of the ants said: "O you ants! Get into your dwellings lest Solomon and his army crush you unawares." (27:17–18)

Islam prohibits cruelty to animals. Thirteen centuries before any societies for prevention of cruelty to animals were established, Islam made kindness to animals a part of its faith, and cruelty to them a sufficient reason for a person to be thrown into the Fire.

Allah's Messenger, upon him be peace and blessings, once related to his Companions that a prostitute found a dog panting with thirst. She descended into a well, filled her shoes with water, and gave it to the dog. She continued to do so until the dog's thirst was quenched. The Messenger said, "Then Allah was pleased with her, forgave her sins, and led her to the way of Paradise."[51] He also mentioned a woman who left a cat without food and drink to die; she was led to the way of Hell.[52]

Respect for Allah's living creatures reached such an extent that when the Messenger saw a donkey with a branded face, he denounced the practice, "I would brand an animal only on the part of its body farthest from its face." Once while returning from a military campaign, a few Companions removed some young birds from their nest to stroke them. The mother bird came back and, not finding her babies, began to fly around screeching. When told of this, Allah's Messenger became angry and ordered the birds to be put back in the nest.[53]

Once he told his Companions that Allah reproached an earlier Prophet for setting fire to a nest of ants.[54] While in Mina, some of his Companions attacked a snake in order to kill it. However, it managed to escape. Watching this from afar, Allah's Messenger remarked, "It was saved from your evil, as you were from its evil."[55] As regards slaughtering animals, Islam insists that it be done in the way that is least painful to the animal and that the knife be sharpened—but not in front of the animal. Ibn 'Abbas reported that Allah's Messenger once saw a man sharpening his knife directly before the sheep to be slaughtered, and asked him, "Do you want to kill it many times?"[56] Islam also prohibits the slaughtering of one animal in front of another.

TRUTHFULNESS AND TRUSTWORTHINESS OR BEING RELIABLE, AND AVOIDING LYING, DECEPTION, AND FALSEHOOD

Being truthful and trustworthy is the cornerstone of being a believer. These qualities are also among the fundamental attributes of Prophethood. No lies or deceit, whether explicit or implicit, were ever heard from the Prophets. The Qur'an declares, *And make mention of Abraham in the Book: He was surely a sincere man of truth, a Prophet* (19:41); *Also make mention of Ishmael in the Book. He was one always true to his promise, and was a Messenger, a Prophet* (19:54); *And mention Idris in the Book. He was surely a sincere man of truth, a Prophet. And We raised him to a high station* (19:56–57). We also read in the Qur'an that a fellow prisoner addressed Prophet Joseph, *Joseph, O man of truth!* (12:46).

The Qur'an orders truthfulness earnestly:

> Pursue, then, what is exactly right (in every matter of the Religion), as you are commanded (by Allah), and those who, along with you, have turned (to Allah with faith, repenting their former ways, let them do likewise); and do not rebel against the bounds of the Straight Path (O believers)! He indeed sees well all that you do. (11:112)

The Prophets had to be and were endowed with truthfulness, for Allah wants everybody to be truthful and extols the truthful, *O you who believe! Keep from disobedience to Allah in reverence for Him and piety, and keep the company of the truthful!* (9:119); and, *Only those are the believers who have truly believed in Allah, and (believed in) His Messenger, then have never since doubted, and who strive hard with their wealth and persons in Allah's cause—those are they who are truthful and honest (in their profession of faith)* (49:15).

The Qur'an praises believers who, without faltering, carry out their promises, *Among the believers are men (of highest valor) who have been true to their covenant with Allah: among them are those who have fulfilled their vow (by remaining steadfast until death), and those who are awaiting (its fulfillment). They have never altered in any way* (33:23).

Allah's Messenger was known as a truthful person even before Islam. The Meccans, even the unbelievers, called him *al-Amin*, the Trustworthy One, the Truthful. Even his enemies did not accuse him of lying after he proclaimed his Prophethood. After the Treaty of Hudaybiya (6 AH), Allah's Messenger sent letters to the rulers of neighboring countries. The Emperor of Byzantium received his letter in Syria at a time when a Meccan trade caravan headed by Abu Sufyan was in the area of Damascus. The Emperor summoned him, and the following conversation took place:

– Do the elite or the weak mostly follow him?
– The weak.

– Has anyone apostatized after converting?

– Not yet.

– Do his followers increase or decrease?

– They increase daily.

– Have you ever heard him tell a lie?

– No, never.

Struck by the answers from Abu Sufyan, who was at that time the most bitter enemy of Islam, the Emperor acknowledged Muhammad's position, "It is inconceivable for one who has never told a lie during his whole life to invent lies against Allah."[57]

Allah's Messenger always encouraged truthfulness, as can be seen in his words as recorded in the following Traditions:

> Promise me six things and I will promise you Paradise: Speak the truth, keep your promises, fulfill your trusts, remain (sexually) chaste, do not look at what is unlawful, and avoid what is forbidden.[58]
>
> Abandon what arouses your suspicions and follow what is certain. Truthfulness gives satisfaction; lying causes suspicion.[59]
>
> Always be truthful, for truthfulness leads to righteousness and righteousness leads to Paradise. If you are always truthful and seek truthfulness, Allah records you as such. Never lie, for lying leads to shamefulness and shamefulness leads to Hell. If you insist on lying and seek deceit, Allah records you as such.[60]

Being a believer implies being a trustworthy person. All Prophets were the best believers and therefore perfect exemplars of trustworthiness. To stress this principle, Allah summarizes the stories of five Prophets using the same words:

> The people of Noah denied (Noah and, thereby, meant to deny all) the Messengers. (Recall) when their brother, Noah, said to them (by way of timely warning): "Will you not keep from disobedience to Allah in reverence for Him, and seek refuge in His protection? Surely I am a Messenger to you, trustworthy. So keep from disobedience to Allah in reverence for Him, and obey me. I ask of you no wage for that (for

conveying Allah's Message); my wage is due only from the
Lord of the worlds.'" (26:105–109).

Replace the name Noah with those of Hud (123–127), Salih
(141–145); Lot (160–164), and Shuʻayb (176–180), and you have
a summarized version of these five Prophets' trustworthiness.

The word *mu'min* (translated as believer) is derived from *amn*,
meaning security, reliability, and a *mu'min* is one trustworthy and
reliable. *Mu'min* is also a Divine Name, for Allah is the ultimate
Mu'min, the source of security and reliability. We put our trust
in, confide in, and rely upon Him. He distinguished the Prophets
by their trustworthiness, and our connection to Him through the
Prophets is based entirely on their trustworthiness and reliability.

Trustworthiness is also an essential quality of Archangel Gabriel. The Qur'an describes Gabriel as one obeyed and trustworthy
(81:21). We received the Qur'an through two trustworthy Messengers: Gabriel and Prophet Muhammad. The former conveyed it; the
latter related it to us.

It should also be added concerning truthfulness or trustworthiness that Islam decisively forbids misusing the truth for worldly
advantages, concealing it where it must be declared, and confound-
ing it with falsehood. Allah knows what people keep concealed and
what they disclose, and it is one of the greatest wrongdoings to
conceal the truth where it must be declared. What follows are some
verses from the Qur'an concerning this matter:

> Do not confound the truth by mixing it with falsehood, and
> do not conceal the truth while you know. (2:42)

> Do they not know that surely Allah knows what they keep
> concealed and what they disclose? (2:77)

> Who is more in the wrong than he who conceals the testimony
> he has from Allah? Allah is never unaware or unmindful of
> what you do. (2:140)

> Those who conceal anything of the clear truths and the
> Guidance that We have sent down, after We have made them

clear in the Book—Allah curses such people (excludes them from His mercy) and so do all who (have any authority to) curse. Except those who repent and mend their ways, and openly declare (those truths and the Guidance)—for those, I return their repentance with forgiveness. I am the One Who accepts repentance and returns it with liberal forgiveness and additional reward, the All-Compassionate. (2:159–160)

FULFILLING TRUSTS

Fulfilling trusts is one of the primary requirements of being a believer or a trustworthy one. The Qur'an orders the believers to deliver trusts to those entitled to them, saying, *Allah commands you to deliver trusts (including public and professional duties of service) to those entitled to them; and when you judge between people, to judge with justice. How excellent is what Allah exhorts you to do. Surely Allah is All-Hearing, All-Seeing* (4:58). A believer must never betray trust. Prophet Joseph, upon him be peace, who did not hesitate to reject the immoral offer of the wife of the Egyptian minister in whose house he had been serving for years, demonstrated to what extent a believer is trustworthy. The Qur'an says:

> And the woman in whose house he was living sought to enjoy herself by him. She bolted the doors and said, "Come, please!" He said: "Allah forbid! My lord (your husband) has given me honorable, good lodging. Assuredly, wrongdoers never prosper." (12:23)

Having preferred staying in prison for years rather than accepting the advance of the wife of the minister, Prophet Joseph once more declared his innocence—his being one who never betrayed trusts—before leaving the prison to be appointed as deputy king or chief minister in Egypt. He said:

> (Joseph was informed of the women's confessions and the declaration of his innocence. He explained why he had asked for the inquiry:) "This was so that he (my former lord) should know that I did not betray him in his absence, and that Allah never guides the schemes of the treacherous (to success)." (12:52)

Trustworthiness or reliability requires strict avoidance of lying, falsehood, breaking one's word and breaching trust. Allah's Messenger, upon him be peace and blessings, said, "The signs of a hypocrite are three: Whenever he speaks, he tells a lie; and whenever he promises, he breaks his promise; and whenever he is entrusted, he betrays (proves to be dishonest)."[61] The Qur'an orders, *So, shun the loathsome evil of idol-worship and shun all words of falsehood!* (22:30) and warns, *Be away from Allah's mercy the liars building on conjecture, who are quite heedless (of truth) in an abyss of ignorance* (51:10–11). The Qur'an praises the believers, saying, *And (those true servants of the All-Merciful are they) who do not take part in, or bear witness to, any vanity or falsehood (and who will not deem anything true unless they know it to be so for certain), and when they happen to pass by anything vain and useless, pass by it with dignity* (25:72).

Allah's Messenger, upon him be peace and blessings, encourages avoidance of lying and warns against it, saying:

> I guarantee a house in the surroundings of Paradise for a man who avoids quarrelling even if he were in the right, a house in the middle of Paradise for a man who avoids lying even if he were joking, and a house in the upper part of Paradise for a man who made his character good.[62]

'Abdullah ibn 'Amir, may Allah be pleased with him, narrates:

> My mother called me one day (when I was a little child). Allah's Messenger, upon him be peace and blessings, was sitting in our house. She told me, "Come here and I shall give you something." Allah's Messenger, upon him be peace and blessings, asked her, "What did you intend to give him?" She replied, "I intended to give him some dates." Allah's Messenger, upon him be peace and blessings, said, "If you were not to give him anything, a lie would be recorded against you."[63]

Allah's Messenger also said, "Whoever does not give up false statements (i.e. telling lies), and evil deeds, and speaking bad words to others, Allah is not in need of his (fasting) leaving his food and drink."[64]

FULFILLING CONTRACTS OR COVENANTS

Islam orders us to fulfill any contract or covenant which we make, or the bonds we enter into. The contract or covenant we make or the bond we enter into may be either with Allah or with people:

> O you who believe! Fulfill the bonds (you have entered into with Allah and with people). (5:1)

> And fulfill Allah's covenant when you have made the covenant (and any commitment that you made among yourselves in Allah's Name), and do not break your oaths after having confirmed them; indeed, you have made Allah your guarantor. Surely Allah knows all that you do. (16:91)

The Qur'an praises believers who fulfill their covenants and are faithful to their trusts or pledges:

> Those who fulfill Allah's covenant (responsible for the order in the universe, and able to establish the peace, order and harmony in human life) and do not break the pledge (that they shall worship none save Allah, and fulfill all the moral, spiritual, and social obligations resulting from believing in and worshipping only One Allah).... (13:20)

> They are faithful and true to their trusts (which either Allah, society, or an individual places in their charge), and to their pledges (between them and Allah or other persons or society). (23:8)

As a requirement for the contracts to be fulfilled, the Qur'an earnestly advises the presence of witnesses and recording them in writing:

> O you who believe! When you contract a debt between you for a fixed term, record it in writing. Let a scribe write it down between you justly, and let no scribe refuse to write it down: as Allah has taught him (through the Qur'an and His

Messenger), so let him write. And let the debtor dictate, and let him avoid disobeying Allah, his Lord, and curtail no part of it. If the debtor be weak of mind or body, or incapable of dictating, let his guardian dictate justly. And call upon two (Muslim) men among you as witnesses.... Let the witnesses not refuse when they are summoned (to give evidence). And (you, O scribes) be not loath to write down (the contract), whether it be small or great, with the term of the contract. Your doing so (O you who believe), is more equitable in the sight of Allah, more upright for testimony, and it is more likely that you will not be in doubt. If it be a matter of buying and selling concluded on the spot, then there will be no blame on you if you do not write it down; but do take witnesses when you settle commercial transactions with one another, and let no harm be done to either scribe or witness (nor let either of them act in a way to injure the parties). If you act (in a way to harm either party, or the scribe and witnesses), indeed it will be transgression on your part. (Always) act in due reverence for Allah and try to attain piety. Allah teaches you (whatever you need in life, and the way you must follow in every matter); Allah has full knowledge of everything. If you are (in circumstances like being) on a journey and cannot find a scribe, then a pledge in hand will suffice. But if you trust one another, let him (the debtor) who is trusted fulfill his trust, and let him act in piety and keep from disobedience to Allah, his Lord (by fulfilling the conditions of the contract). And do not conceal the testimony; he who conceals it, surely his heart (which is the center of faith) is contaminated with sin. Allah has full knowledge of what you do. (2:282–283)

O you who believe! Let there be witnesses among you when death approaches you, at the time of making bequests—two straightforward and trustworthy persons from among your own people (the Muslim community), or two other persons from among people other than your own (from among the People of the Book), if you are on a journey (and there are no Muslims) when the affliction of death befalls you. (5:106)

PRESERVING ONE'S CHASTITY

Islam greatly emphasizes chastity and modesty, considers any unlawful sexual intercourse as a shameful, indecent thing, and an evil
way (leading to individual and social corruption) (17:32), and decisively forbids any indecency:

> Say: "My Lord has made unlawful only indecent, shameful
> deeds (like fornication, adultery, prostitution, and homosexual-
> ity), whether those of them that are apparent and committed
> openly or those that are committed secretly; and any act explic-
> itly sinful; and insolence and offenses (against the Religion,
> life, personal property, others' chastity, and mental and bodily
> health), which is openly unjustified; and (it is also forbidden)
> that you associate partners with Allah, for which He has sent
> no authority at all, and that you speak against Allah the things
> about which you have no sure knowledge. (7:33)

Islam orders people to satisfy their desires and needs in a legitimate manner. They must guard their chastity both by avoiding
all kinds of unlawful sexual relationships and by preserving their
private parts from being exposed. The Qur'an forbids any sexual
relationship not based on a legal (marriage) contract and praises
believers for guarding their chastity and private parts (23:5–7). It
describes other forms of relationships as "seeking beyond (what is
lawful)" (23:7). "Seeking beyond what is lawful" also includes homosexual acts and sex with animals. Imam Malik and Imam Shafi'i
also consider masturbation to be a way of seeking something beyond what is lawful. In addition to certain other vices they had, the
people of Lot were utterly destroyed because of their engagement
in homosexual acts. Prophet Lot, upon him be peace, warned them
for years, saying:

> "What! Do you, of all the world's people, approach men (with
> lust), and leave aside what your Lord has created (and made
> lawful) for you in your wives? No, indeed! You are a people
> exceeding all bounds (of decency)." (26:165–166)

In order to close up the ways to unlawful sexual relationships, the Qur'an also orders as follows:

> Tell the believing men that they should restrain their gaze (from looking at the women whom it is lawful for them to marry, and from others' private parts), and guard their private parts and chastity. This is what is purer for them. Allah is fully aware of all that they do. And tell the believing women that they (also) should restrain their gaze (from looking at the men whom it is lawful for them to marry, and from others' private parts), and guard their private parts, and that they should not display their charms except that which is revealed of itself; and let them draw their veils over their bosoms, and (tell them) not to display their charms to any save their husbands, or their fathers (and grandfathers, and both paternal and maternal uncles), or the fathers of their husbands, or their sons, or the sons of their husbands (both their own and step-sons and grandsons), or their brothers (and foster- and step-brothers), or the sons of their brothers, or the sons of their sisters, or the Muslim women and the women of good conduct with whom they associate, or those (slave-girls) their right hands possess, or the male attendants in their service free of sexual desire, or children that are as yet unaware of femininity. Nor should they stamp their feet (i.e. act in such a manner as to) draw attention to their charms (and arouse the passion of men). And, O believers, turn to Allah all together in repentance that you may attain true prosperity. (24:30–31)

The Qur'an praises Virgin Mary for her chastity, saying, *And (mention) that blessed woman who set the best example in guarding her chastity. We breathed into her out of Our Spirit, and We made her and her son a miraculous sign (of Our Power and matchless way of doing things) for all the worlds.* (21:91)

PIOUS SHYNESS OR MODESTY

Pious shyness or modesty (*haya'*) is one of the great virtues to be found particularly in a believing person. It means that a person refrains from doing things displeasing to Allah in fear and awe of Him. It urges a person to be more careful, more self-possessed and more self-controlled in being mannerly and respectful towards Allah Almighty. Allah Almighty has ingrained bashfulness or shame in human nature. If it is combined with modesty or pious shyness originating in belief in and respect for Allah or in the awareness expressed in verses such as *Does he not know that Allah sees (all things)?* (96:14), and, *Allah is ever watching over you* (4.1), it becomes a great virtue and prevents its owner from committing shameful or indecent acts. If a person is devoid of these feelings or has lost them under the influences of his or her family or environment, it will be difficult to develop them in him or her. Also, if the feeling of shame innate in humankind is not combined with the awareness coming from belief, it cannot last long.

Allah Almighty has forbidden all indecent, shameful deeds:

> Say: "My Lord has made unlawful only indecent, shameful deeds (like fornication, adultery, prostitution, and homosexuality), whether those of them that are apparent and committed openly or those that are committed secretly; and any act explicitly sinful; and insolence and offenses (against the Religion, life, personal property, others' chastity, and mental and bodily health), which is openly unjustified; and (it is also forbidden) that you associate partners with Allah, for which He has sent no authority at all, and that you speak against Allah the things about which you have no sure knowledge." (7:33)

The Prophet, upon him be peace and blessings, was more shy than a virgin in her separate room. If he saw a thing which he disliked, it would be recognized in his face.[65] He said, "Faith has over seventy branches, the most excellent of which is the declaration that there is no deity but Allah, and the humblest of which is the removal of what is injurious from the path; and modesty is a branch of faith."[66] He also said, *"Haya'* (pious shyness or modesty) does not bring anything except good."[67]

The Prophet, upon him be peace and blessings, passed by a man who was admonishing his brother regarding *haya'* and was saying, "You are very shy, and I am afraid that might harm you." Allah's Messenger, upon him be peace and blessings, said to him,

"Leave him, for *haya'* is (a part) of faith."[68] He also said, "One of the sayings of the early Prophets which the people have got is: If you don't feel ashamed, do whatever you like."[69]

A believer's pious shyness should not prevent him or her from learning the rules of the Religion. Allah's Messenger, upon him be peace and blessings, personally answered the particular questions of women, and many times had his wives, particularly 'A'isha, may Allah be pleased with them all, teach them in his place. 'A'isha said about the women of the *Ansar* (Muslims of Medina), "How good are the women of the *Ansar*. Their shyness did not prevent them from learning their religion well."[70]

LENIENCE, GENTLENESS, AND ADOPTING THE WAY OF FORBEARANCE, TOLERANCE, AND FORGIVENESS

Although the Qur'an insists on justice and the equality of rights, and that inviolate values demand equal respect and retribution, it warns against exceeding the limits in retribution, draws attention to the beauty and importance of forgiveness, and exhorts individuals to forgive any wrongdoing inflicted on them. It also strongly advises to repel evil with good:

> These will be granted their reward twice over because they have remained steadfast; and they repel evil with good, and out of what We have provided for them, they spend (in Allah's cause and for the needy, and purely for the good pleasure of Allah). (28:54)

> Goodness and evil can never be equal. Repel evil with what is better (or best). Then see: the one between whom and you there was enmity has become a bosom friend. And none are ever enabled to attain it (such great virtue) save those who are patient (in adversities and against the temptations of their souls and Satan), and none are ever enabled to attain it save those who have a great part in human perfections and virtues. (41:34–35)

The Qur'an also encourages lenience, gentleness, forgiveness, and adopting the way of forbearance and tolerance, and refraining from engaging in hostilities against people:

> It was by a mercy from Allah that (at the time of the setback during the War of Uhud), you (O Messenger) were lenient with them (your Companions). Had you been harsh and hardhearted, they would surely have scattered away from about you. Then pardon them, pray for their forgiveness, and take counsel with them in the affairs (of public concern); and when you are resolved (on a course of action), put your trust in Allah. Surely Allah loves those who put their trust (in Him). (3:159)

> "By Allah," they (Joseph's brothers) responded, "Allah has indeed preferred you above us, and certainly we were sinful." He (Joseph) said: "No reproach this day shall be on you. May Allah forgive you; indeed, He is the Most Merciful of the merciful." (12:91–92)

> (Even so, O Messenger) adopt the way of forbearance and tolerance, and enjoin what is good and right, and withdraw from the ignorant ones (do not care what they say or do). (7:199)

> The (true) servants of the All-Merciful are they who move on the earth gently and humbly, and when the ignorant, foolish ones address them (with insolence or vulgarity, as befits their ignorance and foolishness), they respond with (words of) peace (without engaging in hostility with them). (25:63)

> When they (the believers) hear any vain (useless or aggressive) talk, they turn away from it, without reciprocating it, and say (to those who are engaged in it): "To us are accounted our deeds, and to you, your deeds. Peace be upon you! We do not seek to mix with the ignorant (those unaware of Allah, true guidance and right and wrong)." (28:55)

Anas ibn Malik, may Allah be pleased with him, narrates:

> I served the Prophet, upon him be peace and blessings, at Medina for ten years. I was a boy. Every task that I did was not according to the desire of my master, but he never said to

me, "Fie!"Nor did he say to me, "Why did you do this?" or "Why did you not do this?"[71]

Al-Miqdam ibn Shurayh, quoting his father, said, "I asked 'A'isha about living in the desert. She said, 'Allah's Messenger, upon him be peace and blessings, used to go to the desert to these rivulets. Once he intended to go to the desert and he sent to me a she-camel which had not been used for riding so far. He said to me, "'A'isha! Show gentleness, for if gentleness is found in anything, it beautifies it and when it is taken out from anything it damages it.""[72]

Sa'id ibn al-Musayyab, may Allah be pleased with him, narrates:

> While Allah's Messenger, upon him be peace and blessings, was sitting with some of his Companions, a man reviled Abu Bakr and insulted him. But Abu Bakr remained silent. He insulted him twice, but Abu Bakr controlled himself. He insulted him thrice and Abu Bakr responded to him. Then Allah's Messenger, upon him be peace and blessings, got up when Abu Bakr responded.
>
> Abu Bakr said, "Were you angry with me, Messenger of Allah?" Allah's Messenger, upon him be peace and blessings, replied, "An angel came down from heaven and he was rejecting what he had said to you. When you responded, a devil came. I was not going to sit when the devil came down."[73]

A man came to the Prophet, upon him be peace and blessings, and asked, "Messenger of Allah! How often shall I forgive a servant?" He gave no reply, so the man repeated what he had said, but he still kept silence. When the man asked a third time, he replied, "Forgive him seventy times a day."[74]

Allah's Messenger, upon him be peace and blessings, declared, "Allah loves that one should be kind and lenient in all matters,"[75] and, "He who is deprived of lenience is in fact deprived of good."[76] Allah's Messenger, upon him be peace and blessings, also said:

> No one is more patient than Allah against the harmful saying. He hears from the people that they ascribe children to Him,

yet He gives them health and (supplies them with) provision.[77]

Whenever Allah's Messenger, upon him be peace and blessings, was given the choice of one of two matters, he would choose the easier of the two as long as it was not sinful to do so, but if it was sinful, he would not approach it. Allah's Messenger, upon him be peace and blessings, never took revenge on anybody for his own sake but only when Allah's legal bindings were outraged, in which case he would implement the required sentence.[78]

Allah's Messenger, upon him be peace and blessings, said:

Charity does not in any way decrease wealth; and Allah adds to the respect of the servant who forgives; and the one who shows humility, Allah elevates him in the estimation (of people).[79]

SPEAKING KINDLY AND GOOD WORDS, AND AVOIDING HARSH, DECEPTIVE AND FOUL LANGUAGE

Islam earnestly calls us to speak kindly, and avoid foul language. It warns that through harsh speech, Satan, who is a manifest enemy for humankind, may sow discord among people. The Qur'an says:

> And say to My servants that they should always speak (even when disputing with others) that which is the best. Satan is ever ready to sow discord among them. For Satan indeed is a manifest enemy for humankind. (17:53)

Allah's Messenger, upon him be peace and blessings, warns, "Allah does not like the one who is unseemly and lewd in his language."[80]

We must be especially careful about our language while communicating Islamic truths to people. Allah Almighty ordered Prophets Moses and Aaron, upon them be peace, to speak mildly even to Pharaoh:

> "Go, both of you, to the Pharaoh for he has exceedingly rebelled. But speak to him with gentle words, so that he might reflect and be mindful or feel some awe (of me, and behave with humility)." (20:43–44)

The Qur'an also orders us not to raise our voice and use a respectful language:

> Allah does not like any harsh speech to be uttered save by one who has been wronged (and, therefore, has the right to express that in appropriate language). Allah is indeed All-Hearing, All-Knowing. (4:148)

> Be modest in your bearing, and subdue your voice. For certain, the most repugnant of voices is the braying of donkeys. (31:19)

> O you who believe! Do not say (in your relationship and conversations with Allah's Messenger,) ra'ina (please attend to us), but say, *unzurna* (favor us with your attention), and pay heed to him. (And be assured that) for the unbelievers (who are disrespectful to Allah's Messenger) is a painful punishment. (2:104)

We must always try to speak good, useful words, and be careful that whatever we say should be approvable by Islam:

> Do you not see how Allah strikes a parable of a good word: (a good word is) like a good tree—its roots holding firm (in the ground) and its branches in heaven; it yields its fruit in every season due by its Lord's leave. So Allah strikes parables for human beings, in order that they may reflect on them and infer the necessary lessons. And the parable of a corrupt word is that of a corrupt tree uprooted from upon the earth, having no constancy. (14:24–26)

Our actions should not contradict our words. Allah Almighty severely rebukes those whose words and actions do not accord with each other, saying:

> To Him ascends only the pure word, and the good, righteous action (accompanying it) raises it. But those who are devising evil actions, for them there is a severe punishment, and their devising is bound to come to nothing. (35:10)

> O you who believe! Why do you say what you do not do (as well as what you will not do)? Most odious it is in the sight of Allah that you say what you do not (and will not) do. (61:2–3)

We should be as concise as possible while speaking, and try to avoid uttering words that can be misunderstood. Allah's Messenger, upon him be peace and blessings, spoke in a distinct manner so that anyone who listened to him could understand it, and said, "I have been commanded to be brief in what I say, for brevity is better."[81]

Both the Qur'an and Allah's Messenger, upon him be peace and blessings, warn against false tones and rhythms in speech and using captivating language in order to deceive people. Such styles of speech are signs of hypocrisy:

> Had We so willed, We would have shown them (the hypocrites) to you, and you would have known them by their marks (visible on their faces). But you certainly know them by the false tone and rhythm of their speech. Allah knows (O humankind) your deeds (and why and how you do them). (47:30)

Allah's Messenger, upon him be peace and blessings, said, "Allah, the All-Exalted, hates the eloquent one among men who moves his tongue round (among his teeth), as cattle do."[82]

The Messenger also said, "On the Day of resurrection Allah will not accept repentance or ransom from him who learns excellence of speech to captivate thereby the hearts of men, or of people."[83]

BEING PLEASED WITH OR RESIGNED TO DIVINE DESTINY AND DECREES

Since Allah Almighty is our Creator, as well as the Creator of everything else, He knows us much better than we know ourselves. The Qur'an declares:

> Is it conceivable that One Who creates should not know? He is the All-Subtle (penetrating the most minute dimensions of all things), the All-Aware. (67:14)

This is of great significance. Humans who manufacture something prepare a manual to describe how it must be used, and we use it according to that guide. This means that one who manufactures it knows it best, and that only one who truly knows can manufacture it. So Allah, being the All-Knowing, creates; being the Creator, He knows all that He creates. In addition, while we have no exact knowledge of ourselves, the past, the present, or the future, Allah knows not only us perfectly but also what is to our good and what is to our harm. Being our Creator and Nourisher, He always wills well for believers. Therefore, we must be pleased with or resigned to whatever Allah decrees for us. While encouraging believing men to consort with their wives in a good manner and prescribing fighting for the believers, Allah Almighty reminds us of the same fact that it may well be that we dislike a thing but it is good for us while we like a thing but it is bad for us:

> Prescribed for you is fighting, though it is disliked by you. It may well be that you dislike a thing but it is good for you, and it may well be that you like a thing but it is bad for you. Allah knows, and you do not know. (2:216)

> Consort with them in a good manner, for if you are not pleased with them, it may well be that you dislike something but Allah has set in it much good. (4:19)

As human beings having free will, we are enjoined to follow religious obligations, and cannot ascribe our sins to Allah, nor can our rebellious carnal soul consider itself free of the consequences of its sins by ascribing them to Destiny. On the other hand, Destiny exists so that pious people do not ascribe their good acts to themselves and thereby become proud. Destiny exists so that the successful and the wealthy are not proud of their successes or wealth.

Any past misfortune should be considered in the light of Destiny so that we do not grieve for what has befallen us and what we have not been able obtain. The future, along with sins and questions of responsibility, should be referred to human free will. That is, we should do whatever we must in order to obtain a desired result, and avoid neglect, faults, and sins, while we believe that it is Allah Who creates our deeds. This reconciles the extremes of fatalism and the denial of the role of Destiny in our actions. This also teaches us that we must willingly accept the judgments of Divine Destiny:

> No affliction occurs on the earth (such as droughts, famines, or earthquakes), or in your own persons (such as diseases, damages to your property, or the loss of loved ones), but it is recorded in a Book before We bring it into existence—doing so is surely easy for Allah—so that you may not grieve for what has escaped you, nor exult because of what Allah has granted you: Allah does not love anyone proud and boastful. (57:22–23)

> (O human being!) Whatever good happens to you, it is from Allah; and whatever evil befalls you, it is from yourself. We have sent you (O Messenger) to humankind as a Messenger, and Allah suffices for a witness. (4:79)

Resignation to Divine Destiny also requires that we must never complain of Allah because of any misfortune or failure befalling us but we must complain of our anguish and sorrow to Allah and take shelter in His Mercy and protection:

> He (Jacob) said: "I only complain of my anguish and sorrow to Allah, and I know from Allah what you do not know." (2:86)

Belief in and submission to Allah and Destiny also preserves people from despair, for it is Allah's all-encompassing Mercy Which can always open ways for us out of any difficulty or to any success:

> Do not despair of Allah's Mercy, for none ever despairs of Allah's Mercy, except people who disbelieve in Him." (12:87)

> He (Abraham) said: "Who would despair of his Lord's mercy, other than those who are astray?" (15:56)

Working for Any Intended Goal without Coveting What Others Have

Although it is Allah Almighty Who ultimately gives or takes back, and makes successful or condemns to failure, humans must strive for any intended goal. For human striving or work is included in or taken into consideration by Allah's final judgment to give or not to give or to make successful or unsuccessful. The Qur'an declares:

> And that human has only that for which he labors, and his labor will be brought forth to be seen. (53:39–40)

> And so, whoever does an atom's weight of good will see it; and whoever does an atom's weight of evil will see it. (99:7–8)

Therefore, we must do in lawful ways whatever we must for any aim we intend, but we must not covet what Allah gives others more than us. The Qur'an decrees:

> (People differ from each other in capacity and means of liveli-hood, and it is not in your hands to be born male or female. Therefore) do not covet that in which Allah has made some of you excel others (thus envying others in such things as status or wealth, or physical charms, and so objecting to Allah's dis-tribution). Men shall have a share according to what they have earned (in both material and spiritual terms), and women shall have a share according to what they have earned. (On the other hand, do not refuse effort and aspiration; instead of envying others,) ask Allah (to give you more) of His bounty (through lawful labor and through prayer). Assuredly, Allah has full knowledge of everything. (4:32)

> Or do they envy others for what Allah granted them out of His grace and bounty? Yet We did grant the Family of Abraham (including the progeny of Ishmael proceeding from him, as well as that of Isaac) the Book and the Wisdom, and We granted them a mighty kingdom (in both the material and spiritual realm). (4:54)

See how We have made some of them excel others (in worldly gifts and in virtues); yet the Hereafter will certainly be greater in ranks and greater in excellence. (17:21)

REFRAINING FROM CAUSING DISORDER AND CORRUPTION AND WRONGING PEOPLE

Since the universe obeys or follows the laws established by the One and Single Allah, it has absolute, magnificent order, harmony, and cohesion. What is expected of humanity endowed with free will is to realize the same order, harmony, and cohesion in the human realm by using its free will in obeying Allah. So Islam decisively condemns and forbids causing disorder and corruption and wronging people in any way. Causing disorder and corruption and wronging people are among the principal causes of perdition in both worlds. The following verses of the Qur'an are only some examples of this:

> And to (the people of) Midian, (We sent) their brother, Shu'ayb, as Messenger. He (conveying the same message) said: "O my people! Worship Allah alone: you have no deity other than Him. A manifest proof has assuredly come to you from your Lord. So give full measure and weight (in all your dealings), and do not wrong people by depriving them of what is rightfully theirs, and do not cause disorder and corruption in the land, seeing that it has been so well-ordered. That is for your own good, if you are (to be) true believers. And do not lurk in ambush by every pathway, seeking to overawe and bar from Allah's way one who believes in Him, and seeking to make it appear crooked. (7:85–86)

> But those who break Allah's covenant after its solemn binding, and sever the bonds Allah commanded to be joined, and cause disorder and corruption on the earth—such are those for whom there is curse (exclusion from Allah's mercy), and for them there is the most evil abode. (13:25)

> Give full measure (in all your dealings), and be not one of those who (by cheating and giving less) cause loss to others. And weigh with a true, accurate balance. Do not wrong people by depriving them of what is rightfully theirs, and do not go about acting

wickedly in the land, causing disorder and corruption. (26:181–
183)

Allah forbids all kinds of oppression. The Prophet, upon him
be peace and blessings, warned, "Be on your guard against committing oppression, for oppression is darkness on the Day of
Resurrection"[84]; and, "Allah will punish those who torment people in this world."[85]

REFRAINING FROM FEARING AND HARMING OTHERS

Extremely sensitive about the rights of people, Islam warns against
acts which may injure people or cause fear and alarm in them. Islam
forbids both harming others and returning harm with harm, and
"There is neither giving harm nor returning harm with harm," is
one the fundamental principles of Islamic Law. Allah's Messenger,
upon him be peace and blessings, said:

He who amongst you moves in the mosque or in the bazaar
and there is an arrow with him should take hold of its iron-head in
his palm, so that none amongst the Muslims should receive any injury from it.[86]

None amongst you should point a weapon towards his brother,
for he does not know that Satan might cause the weapon (to slip)
from his hand and (he may injure someone) and thus he may fall
into Hell-fire.[87]

AVOIDING ENVY AND ENVIOUS RIVALRY

The Prophet, upon him be peace and blessings, said, "Avoid envy, for
envy devours good deeds just as fire devours fuel or (he said) grass."[88]

Envying others maliciously for their wealth or achievements
is forbidden in Islam. We can only emulate those who outstrip us
in virtues and good deeds without feeling any malicious envy for
them. The Qur'an orders:

(People differ from each other in capacity and means of livelihood, and it is not in your hands to be born male or female.
Therefore) do not covet that in which Allah has made some of
you excel others (thus envying others in such things as status
or wealth, or physical charms, and so objecting to Allah's dis-
tribution). Men shall have a share according to what they have
earned (in both material and spiritual terms), and women shall
have a share according to what they have earned. (On the
other hand, do not refuse effort and aspiration; instead of
envying others,) ask Allah (to give you more) of His bounty
(through lawful labor and through prayer). Assuredly, Allah
has full knowledge of everything. (4:32)

Malicious envy leads to envious rivalry and insolence, which
has always been the basic factor in people's dividing into opposing
factions. The Qur'an says:

Humankind were (in the beginning) one community (following one way of life without disputing over provision and other
similar things. Later on, differences arose and) Allah sent
Prophets as bearers of glad tidings (of prosperity in return for
faith and righteousness) and warners (against the consequences
of straying and transgression), and He sent down with them
the Book with the truth (containing nothing false in it) so that
it might judge between the people concerning that on which
they were differing. And only those who were given it differed
concerning it, after the most manifest truths came to them,
because of envious rivalry and insolence among themselves.
Allah has guided by His leave those who have believed to the
truth about that on which they were differing. Allah guides
whomever He wills to a straight path. (2:213)

And they (who follow the previous ways) were not divided
(into opposing groups) until after the knowledge came to them
(of the way they must follow and what that entailed, and only)
because of envious rivalry and insolence among themselves.
(42:14)

The (true) religion with Allah is Islam. Those who were given
the Book before differed only after the knowledge (of truth)
came to them because of envious rivalry and insolence among

themselves. Whoever disbelieves in the Revelations of Allah (should know that) Allah is swift at reckoning. (3:19.)

In the early period of human earthly life, people followed a way under the leadership of Prophet Adam, upon him be peace, to whom some Divine Scrolls were reportedly given. There was no rivalry and competition among them about how to share the products of their labor and what the earth yielded. When such competition eventually arose, it resulted in differences, clashes and bloodshed. Allah, out of compassion, raised up Messengers (*rusul*) among them and sent Books with some and Scrolls with some others so that people might live in justice and be guided to the truth in what they differed on. He also raised up Prophets (*anbiya'*) in the footsteps of the Messengers to continue their way. In short, the verses above clarify that the primary reason for the conflicts among the People of the Book, as well as among other peoples, is envious rivalry.

FRIENDSHIP

Anas ibn Malik, may Allah be pleased with him, narrates:

> Allah's Messenger, upon him be peace and blessings, said, "The similitude of good company and that of bad company is that of the owner of musk and of the one (iron-smith) blowing bellows, and the owner of musk would either offer you free of charge or you would buy it from him or you would smell its pleasant odor, and so far as one who blows the bellows is concerned, he would either burn your clothes or you shall have to smell its repugnant smell."[89]

Concerning friendship, Allah's Messenger also said, "A man follows the religion of his friend; so each one should consider with whom he makes his friend."[90]

We must be careful about both choosing our friends and making friends with them. Islam teaches that all Muslims are brothers and sisters, and they should respect, help, and care for each other. One of the important ways to encourage the growth of such affection between people is to visit each other. In this respect Islam has attached great importance to visiting others for the sake of pleasing Allah. The Prophet, upon him be peace and blessings, said, "Whoever visits a sick person or a Muslim for the sake of Allah, a herald shouts, saying, 'Well have you done! May the steps you have taken bring you good, and may your place in Paradise be beautiful!'"[91] Allah's Messenger, upon him be peace and blessings, came to visit Qays ibn Sa'd in his house, stayed for some time, prayed for him, and then left. He would visit the *Ansar*, both individually and as a group. When he visited them individually he went to their homes; when he wanted to see them as a group he would go to the mosque. Once he visited a family from the *Ansar*, ate a meal in their home, offered a Prayer, and prayed for them.[92]

Islam forbids enmity, hatred, and hostility among Muslims. The Qur'an orders mutual helping in virtue and goodness, and piety and righteousness, and forbids mutual helping in sinful, iniquitous acts and hostility (5:2). One of the reasons why it has forbidden intoxicants and games of chance is that through them Satan seeks to provoke enmity and hatred among people: *Satan only seeks to provoke enmity and hatred among you by means of intoxicants and games of chance, and to bar you from the remembrance of Allah and from Prayer. So, then, will you abstain?* (5:91)

Hostilities towards believers cause one to forget Allah's remembrance and perish. What follows is the Qur'anic description of one of the scenes of the Hereafter to be prepared by hostilities towards believers in the world:

> There was among My servants a party who would pray, "Our Lord! We have believed, so forgive us, and have mercy on us, for You are the Best of the merciful." You used to take them in mockery, so much so that your hostilities to them caused you to forget My remembrance, and you simply persisted in laughing at them. But look, today I have rewarded them for what they endured patiently, so that they are those who are the triumphant. (23:109–111)

Concerning friendship among Muslims, Allah's Messenger, upon him be peace and blessings, said, "Do not hate one another, and do not be jealous of one another, and do not desert each other, and O Allah's servants, be brothers (and sisters). It is not lawful for a Muslim to desert (not talk to) his brother (Muslim) for more than three days."[93]

It is stated in another *hadith* narrated by Abu Hurayra, may Allah be pleased with him, that the deeds are presented on every Thursday and Friday and Allah, the All-Glorious, and the person in whose (heart) there is rancor against his brother is not pardoned until they are reconciled.[94]

REFRAINING FROM CURSING OR MALEDICTION

Prophet Muhammad, upon him be peace and blessings, was sent as a mercy for all the worlds, and Islam is a manifestation of Divine mercy throughout. It aims to guide everyone—and guides its true followers—to the truth and true happiness in both worlds. During the War of Uhud, Allah's Messenger, upon him be peace and blessings, was wounded. While his cheek was bleeding, some of his Companions told him to invoke Allah's curse upon those who attacked and wounded him. He answered, "I have not been sent as a curser; I have been sent as a mercy and one to call to the right path." Then he prayed, saying, "O Allah! Show my people to the right path, for they do not know."[95]

Allah's Messenger, upon him be peace and blessings, warned us not to invoke Allah's curse on anything or any being, saying, "Do not invoke Allah's curse, Allah's anger, or Hell."[96]

'Abdullah ibn 'Abbas, may Allah be pleased with him, narrates:

The wind snatched away a man's cloak during the time of the Prophet, upon him be peace and blessings, and he cursed it. The Prophet, upon him be peace and blessings, said, "Do not curse it, for it is under command, and if anyone curses a thing undeservedly, the curse returns upon him."[97]

DOING GOOD TO ALMOST EVERYONE AND REFRAINING FROM HARMING OTHERS

As human beings created of the best stature and as the perfect pattern of creation, we should always prefer goodness. The Qur'an declares:

> Say (O Messenger): "The bad and the good are not alike," even though the abundance of the bad (the sheer quantity of the corrupt) amazes you. So keep from disobedience to Allah in reverence for Him and piety, O people of discernment (so that you may rightly distinguish quality and quantity, and so), that you may prosper (in both worlds). (5:100)

We are social beings compelled to live together with our fellow beings and in need of one another. Harmonious social life requires justice, mutual helping and respect, observation of mutual rights, and giving no one harm. Islam attaches great importance to and earnestly encourages helping others and doing good to almost everyone. It particularly orders treating those under our command or in our service well and kindly. The Qur'an orders:

> And (as the essential basis of contentment in individual, family and social life,) worship Allah and do not associate anything as a partner with Him; and do good to your parents in the best way possible, and to the relatives, orphans, the destitute, the neighbor who is near (in kinship, location, faith), the neighbor who is distant (in kinship and faith), the companion by your side (on the way, in the family, in the workplace, etc.), the wayfarer, and those who are in your service. (Treat them well and bring yourself up to this end, for) Allah does not love those who are conceited and boastful. (4:36)

Concerning how we must treat those in our service, Allah's Messenger, upon him be peace and blessings, declares:

> Your slaves (and servants) are your brothers (or sisters) and
> Allah has put them under your command. So whoever has a
> brother under his command should feed him of what he eats
> and dress him of what he wears. Do not ask them to do things
> beyond their capacity, and if you do so, then help them.[98]

A man came to the Prophet, upon him be peace and blessings, and asked, "Messenger of Allah! How often shall I forgive a servant?" He gave no reply, so the man repeated what he had said, but he still kept silence. When he asked a third time, he replied, "Forgive him seventy times a day."[99]

In many of its verses, the Qur'an calls us to help others, and praises highly those who help others purely for Allah's sake without expecting anything in return from them, while it severely reprimands those who avoid helping others. For example:

> And give his due to the relative, as well as the destitute and the
> wayfarer; and do not squander (your wealth) senselessly.
> Surely squanderers are ever brothers of satans; and Satan is
> ever ungrateful to his Lord. (17:26–27)

> They give food, however great be their need for it, with plea-
> sure to the destitute, and to the orphan, and to the captive,
> (saying): "We feed you only for Allah's sake; we desire from
> you neither recompense nor thanks (we desire only the accep-
> tance of Allah). (76:8–9)

Together with faith, helping others and doing them good are among the most effective ways to be saved from the punishment in the Hereafter:

> What enables you to perceive what the ascent is? It is the free-
> ing of a bondsman (a slave or a captive); or feeding, on a day
> of privation, an orphan near of kin, or a poor wretch in mis-
> ery; and being, besides, of those who believe and exhort one
> another to patience, and exhort one another to pity and com-
> passion. (90:12–17)

The Prophet, upon him be peace and blessings, once mentioned Hellfire and sought refuge with Allah from it, and turned his face away. He mentioned the Hellfire again and took refuge with Allah from it and turned his face away. The Prophet, upon him be peace and blessings, then said, "(O people!) Save yourselves from the Hellfire even if with one half of a date fruit (given in charity), and if this is not available, then (save yourselves) by saying a good, pleasant, friendly word."[100]

Doing people good not only encompasses Muslims but it should also be extended to non-Muslims who are not actively engaged in hostility towards Muslims:

> Allah does not forbid you, as regards those who do not make war against you on account of your Religion, nor drive you away from your homes, to be kindly to them, and act towards them with equity. Allah surely loves the scrupulously equitable. Allah only forbids you, as regards those who make war against you on account of your Religion and drive you away from your homes, or support others to drive you away, to take them for friends and guardians. Whoever takes them for friends and guardians, those are the wrongdoers. (60:8–9)

Allah's Messenger, upon him be peace and blessings, used to run to the aid of everyone, and did not even resist being led by an insane woman to help her. Anas ibn Malik, may Allah be pleased with him, relates that a woman came to Allah's Messenger, upon him be peace and blessings, and said, "Messenger of Allah, I have some need with you." He said to her, "Mother of so-and-so, see on which side of the road you would like (to stand and talk) so that I may fulfill your need for you." He stood aside and talked with her on the roadside until she got what she needed.[101] It happened several times that an old she-slave who was probably insane pulled him by the hand to help her with her housework, and he complied with her request.[102]

We should not be content with doing good to others but carefully refrain from harming them. The Prophet, upon him be peace and blessings, said, "O 'Aisha! The worst people are those whom people desert or leave in order to save themselves from their dirty language or from their transgression."[103]

Unless we avoid doing harm to others, it is really questionable whether our acts of worship such as fasting are acceptable in Allah's sight. Allah's Messenger, upon him be peace and blessings, warns, "Whoever does not give up false statements (i.e. telling lies), and evil deeds, and speaking bad words to others, Allah is not in need of his (fasting) leaving his food and drink."[104]

WHERE GODLINESS LIES

Islam is not composed of certain ceremonial acts. Rather, it is sincerity or purity of intention in belief, sincere worship, and doing good to people purely for Allah's sake or altruism. The Qur'an declares:

> Godliness and virtue is not that you should turn your faces in the direction of the east and west; but he is godly and virtuous who believes in Allah and the Last Day, the angels, the Book, and the Prophets, and gives away of his property with pleasure, although he loves it, to relatives, orphans, the destitute, the wayfarer, and those who have to beg (or who need a loan), and for the liberation of slaves, and establishes the Prayer and pays the Prescribed Purifying Alms. And those (are godly and virtuous) who fulfill their covenant when they have engaged in a covenant, and who are patient and persevering in misfortune, hardship, and disease, and at the time of stress (such as a battle between truth and falsehood). Those are they who are true (in their faith), and those are they who have achieved righteousness, piety, and due reverence for Allah. (2:177)

HASTENING TO VIRTUOUS DEEDS AND STRIVING TOGETHER, AS IF IN A RACE, TOWARDS ALL THAT IS GOOD

The Qur'an encourages Muslims to hasten to all kinds of virtues deeds and strive together towards good as if in a race with each other:

> It is those (illustrious ones) who hasten to do all kinds of virtuous deeds, and they are in a virtuous competition with one another in doing them. (23:61)

Every people have a direction towards which they turn (a goal they turn to in life, and those who turn to the Sacred Mosque have a way they follow to their goal). So strive together, as if in a race (O community of believers), towards all that is good. Wherever you may be, Allah will bring you all together. Surely Allah has full power over everything. (2:148)

RESPONDING TO ANY GOOD DONE TO ONE

The Prophet, upon him be peace and blessings, said, "If someone is given something, he should give something in return for it provided he can afford to; if he cannot afford to, he should mention the one who gave it with his goodness. He who mentions him with his goodness thanks him, and he who conceals is ungrateful to him."[105]

Responding to any good is an important virtue. We read in the Qur'an that when Prophet Moses, upon him be peace, left Egypt and reached the wells of Midian, he watered the flock of two maidens and then the old, respected father of the maidens sent for him in return for the good Moses had done for his daughters:

When he arrived at the wells of Midian, he found there a group of people watering their flocks, and he found, apart from them, two women (maidens) holding back their flock. He said: "What is the matter with you?" The two (women) said: "We do not water our flock until the shepherds take their flocks away. (It is we who do this work because) our father is a very old man." So Moses watered their flock for them; thereafter, one of the two (maidens) approached him, walking bashfully, and said: "My father invites you, so that he may reward you for watering our flock for us." (28:23–25)

Prophet Moses and the old, respected father of the two maidens taught us that we should help those in need and respond to any good done to us.

BEING A MEANS FOR SOMETHING GOOD TO BE DONE

It is a rule that a cause or someone who is a means for something to be done is like its doer. Therefore, Islam exhorts people always to be engaged in doing good or being intermediaries or causes for something good to be done. The Qur'an says:

> Whoever intercedes, mediates or helps for a good cause will have a share in its blessings, and whoever intercedes, mediates or helps for an evil cause shares in its burden. Allah has full watch over all things. (4:85)

Concerning the same point, Allah's Messenger, upon him be peace and blessings, says:

> Those who establish a good path in Islam receive the reward of those who follow it, without any decrease in their reward. Those who establish an evil path in Islam are burdened with the sins of those who follow it, without any decrease in their burden."[106]

OBSERVING THE RIGHTS OF NEIGHBORS

Islam wants its followers to give a hand to as many people as possible or extend their area of doing good as widely as possible. Neighbors are among the people to whom we must give priority in doing good and whose rights we must observe. Here we can mention once more the Qur'an's order concerning doing good to people:

> And (as the essential basis of contentment in individual, family and social life,) worship Allah and do not associate anything as a partner with Him; and do good to your parents in the best way possible, and to the relatives, orphans, the destitute, the neighbor who is near (in kinship, location, faith), the neighbor who is distant (in kinship and faith), the companion by your side (on the way, in the family, in the workplace, etc.), the wayfarer, and those who are in your service. (Treat them well and bring yourself up to this end, for) Allah does not love those who are conceited and boastful. (4:36)

'Abdullah ibn 'Amr had a sheep slaughtered and said (to his family), "Have you presented a gift from it to my neighbor, the Jew, for I heard Allah's Messenger, upon him be peace and blessings, say, 'Gabriel kept on recommending me about treating the neighbors kindly, so much so that I thought he would make them my heirs."¹⁰⁷

One's neighbors are not only those in adjoining houses, but everyone living nearby, up to forty doors away— including non-Muslims. We should not eat and go to bed when a neighbor is hungry. We should visit them on certain occasions like the *'Iyds*, and especially when they are ill; when they ask for any help, we should give it; we should cover their faults; we should never give them trouble; and when they die, we should attend their funeral.

Allah's Messenger, upon him be peace and blessings, warns against neglecting one's duties towards one's neighbors, saying, "One who goes to bed full while one's neighbor is hungry cannot belong to us."¹⁰⁸ He also said, "Anybody who believes in Allah and the Last Day should not harm his neighbor, and anybody who believes in Allah and the Last Day should entertain his guest generously and anybody who believes in Allah and the Last Day should say what is good or keep quiet."¹⁰⁹

One who knowingly neglects to care for neighbors in need can have only a superficial faith. It must not be forgotten that the Prophet also warned, "Wherever someone goes hungry, his neighborhood will answer to Allah for it."¹¹⁰

Abu Dharr, may Allah be pleased with him, narrates, "Allah's Messenger, upon him be peace and blessings, recommended to me, 'When you make some broth, add extra water to it, and have in your mind the members of the household of your neighbors and then give them out of this with courtesy.'"¹¹¹

We must be careful about not doing any harm to our neighbors. The Prophet, upon him be peace and blessings, said, "By Allah, he does not believe! By Allah, he does not believe! By Allah, he does not believe!" It was said, "Who is that, O Allah's Messenger?" He said, "That person whose neighbor does not feel safe from his evil."¹¹² According to Muslim's record, the Messenger said, "He will not enter Paradise whose neighbor is not secure from his wrongful conduct."¹¹³

Feeding and Helping Orphans, Widows, and the Destitute

Islam attaches great importance to helping the needy, and especially to providing food, clothing, and sheltering for orphans, widows, and the destitute, or those who have no one to care for them. When the Messenger received the first Revelation in the cave of Hira in Mount Nur near Mecca and told his wife Khadija about it in anxiety, Khadija, Mother of Believers, may Allah be pleased with her, calmed him, saying, "Allah will never disgrace you. You keep good relations with your kith and kin, help the poor and the destitute, serve your guests generously, and assist the deserving calamity-afflicted ones."[114]

The Qur'an insistently calls on the believers to care for orphans, and the destitute. For example:

> And do not draw near to the property of the orphan except in the best way (such as to improve and increase it) until he comes of age and is strong; and fulfill the covenant: the covenant is surely subject to questioning (on the Day of Judgment, you will be held accountable for your covenant). (17:34)

> Do not give to those of weak mind your property that Allah has put in your charge (as a means of support for you and for the needy), but feed and clothe them out of it (especially with the profit you will make by exploiting it), and speak to them in a kindly way and with words of honest advice. (Care for and) test the orphans well until they reach the age of marriage. Then, if you find them to be mature of mind, hand over to them their property; and do not consume it by wasteful spending, nor do so in haste, fearing that they will come of age (and so take it over). If the guardian is rich (enough to support himself and his family), let him abstain (from his ward's property); but if he is poor, let him consume thereof in a just and reasonable manner. When you hand (their property) over to them, let there be witnesses on their behalf. Allah suffices as One Who reckons and settles the accounts (of His servants). (4:5–6)

Therefore, do not oppress the orphan; nor chide and drive away the petitioner. (93:9–10)

The Qur'an advises believers to make use of every opportunity to help orphans and the destitute. For example, it exhorts them to give them something out of the inheritance if they are present at its division:

If some from among other relatives (who do not have a legally defined share), and orphans and the destitute, are present at the division (of the inheritance), give them something thereof (for their provision), and speak to them kindly and pleasing words. (4:8)

In observing the rights of orphans, the Qur'an advises believers to consider how they would like the vulnerable offspring they may leave behind to be treated:

Let those be anxious (for the rights of the orphans) who, if they (themselves) were to leave behind weak offspring, would be fearful on their account—and let them keep from disobedience to Allah for fear of His punishment, and let them speak the truth and proper words (in respect of the division of the inheritance and their treatment of the orphans). Surely those who consume the property of orphans wrongfully, certainly they consume a fire in their bellies; and soon they will be roasting in a Blaze (the like of which you have never seen, and the degree of whose intensity none knows except Allah). (4:9–10)

Feeding orphans or the destitute is a means for climbing the ascents on the way to Paradise:

What enables you to perceive what the ascent is? It is the freeing of a bondsman (a slave or a captive); or feeding, on a day of privation, an orphan near of kin, or a poor wretch in misery; and being, besides, of those who believe and exhort one another to patience, and exhort one another to pity and compassion. (90:12–17)

Allah's Messenger, upon him be peace and blessings, said, "I and the person who looks after an orphan and provides for him, will be in Paradise like this," putting his index and middle fingers together.[115]

He also said, "The one who looks after and works for a widow and for a poor person, is like a warrior fighting for Allah's cause or like a person who fasts during the day and prays all the night."[116]

SPREADING ONE'S WINGS OF COMPASSION AND GENEROSITY OVER THE POOR AND WEAK

Islam, which attaches great importance to social unity and solidarity and fellowship among people, exhorts its followers to spread their wings of compassion and generosity over the poor and weak or to provide care and shelter for them. This matter is so important that the leading, rebellious elite among the peoples of many Prophets scorned the weak and poor and detested being together with them. They opposed the Prophets because the poor and weak believed in them and were in their company, and stipulated that the Prophets should drive them away if they wanted them (the rebellious elite) to believe. However, the Prophets never agreed with them, and Allah ordered them to keep company with the poor, humble believers, and spread their wings over them. The following verses are examples of this:

> And do not (in the hope of persuading the chieftains of the unbelievers) drive away any of those (poor believers of humble social standing) who, in the morning and afternoon, invoke their Lord, seeking His "Face" (i.e. the meeting with Him Hereafter and His eternal, good pleasure). You are not accountable for them in anything, just as they are not accountable for you in anything, that you should drive them away, and so become among the wrongdoers. And it is in this way that We try people through one another: so that they (who think that such things as wealth and social status are the means of superiority) say (of the believers who are poor and lacking in recognized social status): "Are these the ones among us on whom Allah has bestowed His favor?" Does Allah not know best who

are the thankful (who recognize the real source and bestower of
every good thing one receives, and act accordingly)? (6:52–53)

And keep yourself patient, along with those who invoke their
Lord morning and evening, seeking His "Face" (His eternal,
good pleasure, and the meeting with Him in the Hereafter);
and do not let your eyes pass beyond them, desiring the beauties of the life of this world (by the participation of those of
leading positions among people in your assemblies). And pay
no heed to (the desires of) him whose heart We have made
unmindful of Our remembrance, who follows his lusts and fancies, and whose affair exceeds all bounds (of right and decency).
(18:28)

The leading ones who disbelieved from among his (Noah's)
people said: "We do not see you but as a mortal like ourselves,
and we do not see that any follow you save those who are but
the lowliest of us, without an opinion worthy of consideration;
and we do not see you (and your followers) having any superiority over us; rather, we take the view that you are liars."
(11:27) "Shall we believe in you, when the lowliest (among
the people) follow you!" (Noah) said: "What knowledge could
I have about what they were engaged in doing (before they
became believers)? Indeed their reckoning rests with none but
my Lord; if only you could understand! And it is not expected
of me that I should repel the believers." (26:111–114)

Spread your wings (to provide care and shelter) over the
believers who follow you (in practicing Allah's commandments
in their lives). (26:215)

BEING GENEROUS BUT REFRAINING FROM WASTEFULNESS

Both the Qur'an and Allah's Messenger, upon him be peace and
blessings, encourage generosity and magnanimity, and condemn
niggardliness. They also call us to avoid wastefulness. The best is
the middle way between wastefulness and niggardliness:

And give his due to the relative, as well as the destitute and the
wayfarer; and do not squander (your wealth) senselessly.
Surely squanderers are ever brothers of satans; and Satan is
ever ungrateful to his Lord. Do not keep your hand bound to

your neck (in niggardliness), nor stretch it without any restraint, or else you will be left sitting reproached and denuded. Surely your Lord Allah enlarges provision for whom He wills, and straitens it (for whom He wills). Indeed He is fully aware of His servants and sees them well. (17:26–27, 29–30)

And who, when they spend (both for their own and others' needs), are neither wasteful nor niggardly, and (are aware that) there is a happy mean between those (two extremes). (25:67)

Spending must be either to meet a necessity or a need, or to satisfy a desire for lawful beauty. Eating to maintain life is a necessity; eating to be full—provided that one avoids excess—is a need; eating pleasant food satisfies one's desire for beauty. Spending in order to meet a necessity is obligatory; meeting a need is commendable, while satisfying one's desire for beauty may be harmless, according to the general conditions of the community and one's income. Spending in order to obtain an easy life while the majority of the Muslims are in need is wastefulness. Islam advises, encourages, and calls to a moderate life and economy in spending, and exhorts us to refrain from luxury. It also orders spending in Allah's cause and for the needy. Allah's Messenger says that the property we truly possess is that which we have forwarded to the eternal world (by spending it in Allah's cause or for the needy), while the property we have left behind after our death belongs to our inheritors.[117]

Spending on unlawful things, no matter the amount, and overspending on lawful things, in the sense that one spends more than one can afford or one aspires to a luxurious life, are also included under the idea of wastefulness. As for niggardliness, this means spending too little on the necessities and needs of oneself and one's family, even though one has sufficient funds, or the refusal to spend on charity or for the cause of Islam.

Allah's Messenger, upon him be peace and blessings, was matchless in generosity. Jabir ibn 'Abdullah says, "Never was the Prophet, upon him be peace and blessings, asked to give a thing for which his answer was 'No!'"[118]

Allah's Messenger warned against niggardliness. He said, "Shall I inform you about the inmates of Hellfire? They are all proud, mean and haughty."[119] He also said that bad morals or evil nature and niggardliness are not to be found in a believer,[120] and that neither a rich, mean or niggardly one nor a rude, hard-hearted one can enter Paradise.[121]

A man asked the Prophet, "O Messenger of Allah! What kind of charity is the best?" He replied, "Giving in charity when you are healthy and greedy hoping to be wealthy and afraid of becoming poor. Don't delay giving in charity till the time when you are on your death bed when you say, 'Give so much to so and so and so much to so-and-so,' and at that time the property is not yours but it belongs to so and so (i.e. your inheritors)."[122]

ENTERTAINING ONE'S GUESTS GENEROUSLY

Generosity is one of the greatest virtues earnestly encouraged and praised by the Qur'an. Entertaining one's guests generously is a great virtue connected with generosity. In several of its verses (i.e., 2:177; 4:36; 17:26), the Qur'an orders providing food and shelter for needy wayfarers, and giving them financial help so that they can reach their destination.

We read in the Qur'an that when Allah's heavenly envoys came to Prophet Abraham in human form to give him the glad tidings that his old wife Sarah would give him a son, Prophet Abraham, upon him be peace and blessings, brought them a roasted calf without delay (11:69; 51:26).

Allah's Messenger, upon him be peace and blessings, said, "Anyone who believes in Allah and the Last Day should not harm his neighbor, and anyone who believes in Allah and the Last Day should entertain his guest generously and anyone who believes in Allah and the Last Day should say what is good or keep quiet."[123]

The Messenger taught us how we should treat our guests and how guests should behave, saying, "Whoever believes in Allah and the Last Day, should serve his guest generously. Serving the guest generously is to provide him with a superior type of food for a night and a day, and a guest is to be entertained with food for three days. Whatever is offered beyond that is regarded as something given in charity. And it is not lawful for a guest to stay with his host for such a long period as to put him in a critical position."[124]

EATING IN ONE ANOTHER'S HOUSE

Islam, which greatly encourages mutual helping and solidarity in society and answering the invitation of believers, and which attaches great importance to caring for the destitute, orphans, and widows, gives permission to believers to eat in the houses of their relatives and close friends. It also permits those who are unable to provide for themselves and have no one to look after them to eat in the house of any wealthy person. The Qur'an declares:

> There is no blame on the blind, nor any blame on the lame, nor any blame on the sick (for eating only to satisfy their need without causing any harm and waste, in the house of any healthy, well-off person), and neither on yourselves, that (in case of need and without prior invitation) you eat in your spouse's and children's houses, or your fathers' houses, or your mothers' houses, or your brothers' houses, or your sisters' houses, or your paternal uncles' houses, or your paternal aunts' houses, or your maternal uncles' houses, or your maternal aunts' houses, or in the houses for which you are responsible, or in the houses of any of your close friends (who should be happy to see you feeling free to eat at their home). There is no blame on you if you eat together or separately. But when you enter any of these houses, greet one another with a blessed, pure and good salutation appointed by Allah. Thus, Allah makes clear for you (the instructions in) His Revelations, that you may reason and understand. (24:61)

ANSWERING INVITATIONS

Believers should answer the invitations of one another. Allah's Messenger, upon him be peace and blessings, would accept the gifts given to him and answered invitations.[125] Once he said, "If I am given a gift so much as a sheep's calf, I accept it; and if I am invited to a meal where even a sheep's calf is offered, I answer it."[126]

The Messenger, upon him be peace and blessings, advised, "If someone asks you for asylum, give him asylum; if someone begs in Allah's name, give him something; if someone invites you to something, answer him; if someone does you some good, return it, but if you do not have the means to do so, then pray for him until you feel that you have compensated him."[127]

The following verse, which describes how the Companions were expected to act when they were invited by the Prophet to a meal, upon him be peace and blessings, is also a guide for the believers concerning how they should act when they are invited to a meal:

> O you who believe! Do not enter the Prophet's rooms (in his house) unless you have been given leave, (and when invited) to a meal, without waiting for the proper time (when the meal is to be served). Rather, when you are invited, enter (his private rooms) at the proper time; and when you have had your meal, disperse. Do not linger for mere talk. That causes trouble for the Prophet, and he is shy of (asking) you (to leave). But Allah does not shy away from (teaching you) the truth. When you ask something of them (his wives), ask them from behind a screen. Your doing so is purer for your hearts and for their hearts. It is not for you to cause hurt to Allah's Messenger, as it is unlawful for you ever to marry his widows after him. That (marrying his widows) would be an enormity in Allah's sight. (33:53)

REFRAINING FROM BEING A BURDEN UPON OTHERS

Although Islam encourages and orders altruism, individual sacrifice, mutual helping, and social solidarity, it discourages begging and being a burden from others. Having the necessary provision for the pilgrimage is one of its prerequisites. The Qur'an orders, *Take your provisions for the Hajj (and do not be a burden upon others)* (2:197).

There may always be beggars who are in desperate need, and helping them is a religious, humanitarian duty. A man came to Ibn 'Abbas to beg for something. Ibn 'Abbas asked him if he bore witness to the Oneness of Allah and the Messengership of Muhammad, upon him be peace and blessings. The man replied affirmatively. Ibn 'Abbas asked him whether he fasted. When the man also gave an affirmative answer to this question, Ibn 'Abbas said, "You asked for something. One who asks has a right, and it is a duty upon us to give one who asks," and gave the man a garment." Then Ibn 'Abbas remarked, "I heard Allah's Messenger, upon him be peace and blessings, saying, 'A Muslim who provides another Muslim with a garment is under Allah's protection so long something of that garment is on him.'"[128]

However, Islam never approves of the begging of a poor, needy person able to work to earn their living. Anas ibn Malik, may Allah be pleased with him, narrates:

A man of the *Ansar* came to the Prophet, upon him be peace and blessings, and begged from him. The Prophet asked, "Don't you have anything in your house?" He replied, "Yes, a piece of cloth, a part of which we wear and a part of which we spread (on the ground), and a wooden bowl from which we drink water."

The Prophet, upon him be peace and blessings, said, "Bring them to me." He then brought these articles to him and the Prophet took them in his hands and asked, "Who will buy these?" A man said, "I will buy them for one *dirham*." The Prophet said twice or thrice, "Who will offer more than one *dirham*?" A man said, "I will buy them for two *dirhams*."

The Prophet, upon him be peace and blessings, gave these to him and took the two *dirhams* and, giving them to the *Ansari*, he said, "Buy food with one of them and offer it to your family, and buy an axe and bring it to me." He then brought it to him. Allah's Messenger, upon him be peace and blessings, fixed a handle on it with his own hands and said, "Go, gather firewood and sell it, and do not let me see you for a fortnight." The man went away and gathered firewood and sold it. When he had earned ten *dirhams*, he came to the Prophet, having bought a garment with some of them and food with the others.

Allah's Messenger, upon him be peace and blessings, then said, "This is better for you than that begging should come as a spot on your face on the Day of Judgment. Begging is right only for three people: one who is in grinding poverty, one who is seriously in debt, or one who is responsible for compensation and finds it difficult to pay."[129]

VISITING THE SICK

One of the duties or rights to be observed among Muslims is that when a Muslim becomes sick, others must visit him or her.[130] Visitors stay for some time—not so long as to bore or bother him or her—with the sick one, and pray to Allah for him or her.

Concerning the merit of visiting the sick, Allah's Messenger, upon him be peace and blessings, said, "The one who visits the sick is in fact like one who is in a garden of Paradise so long as he stays there."[131]

In another *hadith*, Allah's Messenger said:

> Allah, the All-Exalted and Glorious, will say on the Day of Resurrection: "O son of Adam, I was sick but you did not visit Me." He will say: "O my Lord, how could I have visited You while You are the Lord of the worlds?" Thereupon He will say: "Didn't you know that such and such servant of Mine was sick but you did not visit him; were you not aware that if you had visited him, you would have found Me by him? O son of Adam, I asked you for food but you did not feed Me." He will say: "My Lord, how could I have fed You while You are the Lord of the worlds?" He will say: "Didn't you know that such and such servant of Mine asked you for food but you did not feed him; were you not aware that if you had fed him you would have found Me by him?" (The Lord will again say:) "O son of Adam, I asked you for drink but you did not provide Me." He will say: "My Lord, how could I have provided You while You are the Lord of the worlds?" Thereupon He will say: "Such and such servant of Mine asked you for a drink but you did not provide him, and had you provided him drink you would have found Me by him."[132]

CONSULTATION

Consultation is indispensable to the life of Muslims. The opinion of those who are learned, pious, and have sound judgment and expert knowledge, in addition to enjoying the people's confidence, is to be sought. In turn, those people are expected to express their opinions, according to the dictates of their conscience, with precision and integrity. Consultation is so important in the life of Muslims that Allah praises the first, exemplary Muslim community as one whose affair is by counsel among them:

> And those who answer the call of their Lord and obey Him (in His orders and prohibitions), and establish the Prayer in conformity with its conditions; and whose affairs are by consultation among themselves; and who spend out of what We provide for them (to provide sustenance for the needy, and in Allah's cause). (42:38)

Consultation is the first requirement for reaching the right decision. Decisions reached without due reflection or proper consultation usually come to nothing. Individuals who depend only on themselves are disconnected from others and unconcerned with the opinions of others; such people, even if they happen to be geniuses, are at considerable risk of error, as compared to those who exchange opinions and arguments.[133]

This importance of consultation becomes more explicit when the Prophet's leadership is considered. Although he never spoke out of caprice and on his own authority, but only spoke what Allah revealed (53:3–4), Allah ordered him to consult with his Companions (3:159). Even after the Muslims' reverse at the Battle of Uhud (in 625), due to some of the Companions' disobedience to the Prophet's orders, Allah told him to engage in consultation. The Prophet, upon him be peace and blessings, and his rightly-guided successors always followed the principle of consultation.

Good Manners or Acceptable Observances and Practices in Assemblies or Gatherings

We find detailed information about how we should behave when we are together with other people.

The first thing to be observed is that we must come together or hold gatherings only for virtue, goodness, righteousness and piety, not sinful, iniquitous acts and hostility. For the Qur'an orders:

> Help one another in virtue and goodness, and righteousness and piety, and do not help one another in sinful, iniquitous acts and hostility; (in all your actions) keep from disobedience to Allah in reverence for Him and piety. (5:2)

We must refrain from secret talks in gatherings. The Prophet, upon him be peace and blessings, warns, "When you are three people in a place, let two of you not talk to each other secretly."[134] As we must refrain from any secret talks in gatherings, in addition to refraining from any talks made for sin, iniquity, and conspiracy, we must also avoid holding gatherings for the same aims. Any talk or gathering must be for either charity or kind equitable dealings and honest affairs or setting things right between people, or for virtue, goodness, righteousness and piety.

> No good is there in most of their secret talks and counsels except for him who exhorts to a deed of charity, or kind equitable dealings and honest affairs, or setting things right between people. Whoever does that seeking Allah's good pleasure, We will grant to him a tremendous reward. (4:114)

> Have you not considered those who were forbidden to hold secret counsels, and yet reverted to what they had been forbidden, and held secret counsels to commit sins (such as drinking alcohol, gambling, and evading the Prayer), and for (urging one another to) offensiveness and disobedience to the Messenger (in his commands and prohibitions). O you who believe! If you hold secret counsels, do not hold secret counsels to commit sins, or for (urging one another to) offensiveness, or disobedience to the Messenger; but rather, hold counsels for godliness, and righ-

teousness, and piety. Keep from disobedience to Allah in reverence for Him and piety, to Whom you will be gathered.
(58:8–9)

We must greet those present both when we come to an assembly and when we leave it. The Prophet, upon him be peace and
blessings, said, "When one of you comes to an assembly, he should
give a salutation and if he feels inclined to get up, he should give a
salutation, for the former is not more of a duty than the latter."[135]

When we enter a place where there are people, we must sit down
where there is room, and refrain from sitting between two people without their permission. Jabir ibn Samura, may Allah be pleased with
him, narrates, "When we came to the Prophet, upon him be peace
and blessings, each one would sit down where there was room.[136] The
Prophet said, "It is not permissible that a person sits between two people without their permission."[137]

We must make room for a newcomer while we are in an assembly, and we must leave it when it is time for us to leave. Besides, we
must act as deliberately as possible and our acts must be based on
knowledge. The Qur'an orders:

> O you who believe! When you are told, "Make room in the
> assemblies (for one another, and for newcomers)," do make
> room. Allah will make room for you (in His grace and
> Paradise). And when you are told, "Rise up (and leave the
> assembly)," then do rise up. Allah will raise (in degree) those
> of you who truly believe (and act accordingly), and in degrees,
> those who have been granted the knowledge (especially of reli-
> gious matters). Surely Allah is fully aware of all that you do.
> (58:11)

Whenever Muslims or those among them who are concerned
are summoned to a collective cause, they should never fail to respond to the call nor depart without the permission of the ruler,
leader or administrator. Should any of them have a reason for de-
parting, the reason must be a genuine, valid one, and again, they
should not depart without permission. The administrator or leader

is fully entitled to grant or deny the permission that has been asked for, at his discretion. The Qur'an declares:

> Only those are true believers who believe in Allah and His Messenger, and who, when they are with him for a collective cause, do not leave unless they have obtained his permission. Surely those who ask for your permission, it is they who truly believe in Allah and His Messenger. So, if they ask you for permission for some affair of their own, give permission to whomever of them you will, and ask Allah for forgiveness on their behalf. Surely, Allah is All-Forgiving, All-Compassionate. (4:62)

Allah's Messenger, upon him be peace and blessings, forbade standing up for anyone no matter how respectable he or she is. Although the Companions loved Allah's Messenger wholeheartedly, they did not stand up when he entered upon them because they knew that he did not like them to do so. He said, "One who likes that people stand up for him should be prepared for his place in the Fire."[138]

Another point to note concerning the good manners or rules to observe in assemblies is what is pronounced in the following *hadith*:

It is not proper that one is led in the Prayer where he is authorized to lead the Prayer, and no one should sit on a person's chair without his permission.[139]

REFRAINING FROM SWEARING MUCH, AND BEING MINDFUL OF OATHS SWORN

Islam does not approve of swearing much, for swearing brings responsibility. Swearing is not something to take lightly, so when people have sworn once, they must be mindful of their oaths. Breaking one's oath requires expiation. The Qur'an orders:

> And fulfill Allah's covenant when you have made the covenant (and any commitment that you made among yourselves in Allah's Name), and do not break your oaths after having confirmed them; indeed, you have made Allah your guarantor. Surely Allah knows all that you do. (16:91)

Allah does not take you to task for a slip (or blunder of speech) in your oaths, but He takes you to task for what you have concluded by solemn, deliberate oaths. The expiation (for breaking such oaths) is to feed ten destitute persons (or one person for ten days) with the average of the food you serve to your families, or to clothe them, or to set free a slave. If anyone does not find (the means to do that), let him fast for three days. That is the expiation for your oaths when you have sworn (and broken them). But be mindful of your oaths (do not make them lightly, and when you have sworn them, fulfill them). Thus Allah makes clear to you His Revelations (the lights of His way), that you may give thanks (from the heart and in speech, and in action by fulfilling His commandments). (5:89)

We must especially refrain from making our oaths a means of deceiving and wronging others, and screening our misdeeds and barring people from the right way:

Do not make your oaths a means of deception and wrongdoing among yourselves, lest feet should slip (from the way of guidance) after having been firm (on it, and that others, too, may be misled by your misconduct); and you should taste the evil (consequences) of your barring from Allah's way. And (in the Hereafter) there is a mighty punishment for you. (16:94)

They take their oaths as a covering (to screen their misdeeds and themselves from accusation), and bar (people) from Allah's way. Therefore, there is for them a humiliating punishment. (58:16)

Misusing oaths as a shelter to hide conspiracy or ill will and bar people from the right way is a sign of hypocrisy and particular to hypocrites:

They make their oaths a shelter (to hide their inner unbelief and protect themselves in the Muslim community), and so divert themselves (and seek to bar others) from Allah's way. Evil indeed is what they habitually do. (63:2)

REFRAINING FROM DISCLOSING SINS COMMITTED SECRETLY

Believers must avoid committing a sin as much as possible. However, considering that humans are fallible by nature, when they fall or commit a sin in secret, they must never disclose it to people. They must repent for it, keep it secret, and ask for Allah's forgiveness for it. Allah's Messenger, upon him be peace and blessings, said:

All the sins of my followers are forgivable except the sins of those who commit a sin openly or disclose their sins to people. An example of such disclosure is that a person commits a sin at night and though Allah screens it from the public, then he comes in the morning, and says, "O so and so, I did such and such (evil) deed yesterday," though he spent his night screened by his Lord and in the morning he removes Allah's screen from himself.[140]

GREETING WITH THE GREETING OF ISLAM

Spreading greeting among Muslims is very important. Allah's Messenger, upon him be peace and blessings, who greeted or saluted even children playing,[141] says:

Without faith you cannot enter Heaven. And without loving each other you cannot have faith. Shall I show you something to do out of love for each other? Spread greeting among you.[142]

The Prophet, upon him be peace and blessings, who mentioned providing food and extending greetings to those whom one knows or does not know as being among the most meritorious acts in Islam,[143] also says:

Six are the rights of a Muslim over another Muslim: When you meet him, offer him greetings; when he invites you to a feast accept it. When he seeks your counsel give it to him, and when he sneezes and says, *al-hamdu lillah* ("All praise is for Allah,") say *Yarhamuka'llah* ("May Allah show you mercy"); and when he falls ill visit him; and when he dies follow his funeral bier.[144]

According to the Prophet's decree, the rider should first greet the pedestrian, and the pedestrian the one who is seated and a small group should greet a larger group.[145] However, the Prophet also encourages being the first to greet. He says, "Those who are nearest to Allah are they who are first to give a salutation."[146]

The Qur'an, which relates that when Allah's heavenly envoys went to Abraham in human form to give him the glad tidings that he would have a son, they greeted him (11:69), orders us not to enter a house without greeting its residents (24:27). In the pre-Islamic age of *Jahiliyya*, people would barge into each other's houses without asking for permission or greeting the residents with peace, only saying, "Good morning!" or "Good evening!" Islam ruled that everyone has a right to privacy in their own houses, and that no one could enter another's house without ascertaining the prior consent of the residents. Islam also ruled that the proper way to greet one another is not to say anything meaning greeting but to give the salutation Allah appointed or prescribed: *When you enter any of these houses, greet one another with a blessed, pure and good salutation appointed by Allah. Thus, Allah makes clear for you (the instructions in) His Revelations, that you may reason and understand* (24:61). This salutation is prescribed in a *hadith* as follows:

> When a Muslim greets another Muslim this way (*Salamun alaykum*, meaning, "Peace be upon you!"), the response is, "*Wa alaykum salam wa rahmatullah!*" (meaning, "And may peace and the mercy of Allah be upon you!"). And if the first greeting was, *salamun alaykum wa rahmatullah* ("Peace and the mercy of Allah be on you,") the response is, "*Wa alaykum salam wa rahmatullahi wa barakatuh!*" ("And may peace, Allah's mercy and blessings be upon you!").

The Messenger, upon him be peace and blessings, taught that this last form of the greeting was the one used between Prophet Adam, the first man, and the angels.[147] This *hadith* explains the following verse:

> When (whether traveling or at home, or in war or at peace) you are greeted with a greeting, answer with one better, or (at least) with the same. Surely Allah keeps account of all things. (4:86)

Giving the salutation prescribed by Allah is a sign of being a Muslim. Therefore, during a military expedition, the Qur'an forbids killing one who greets with this greeting without investigating and clarifying the situation fully:

> O you who believe! When you go forth (to war) in Allah's cause, investigate with care until the situation becomes fully clear to you, and do not say to anyone who offers you the greeting (appointed by Allah and thereby indicating his being a Muslim), "You are not a believer," seeking the fleeting gains of the present, worldly life; for with Allah are gains abundant. Even thus (as he now is) were you before (ignorant of faith and what being a Muslim is, and you, too, entered Islam with a similar word); but Allah has since then been gracious to you. So investigate with care until the situation becomes fully clear to you. Surely Allah is fully aware of all that you do. (4:94)

REFRAINING FROM SHOW AND OSTENTATION

Since sincerity or purity of intention is the spirit and foundation of any good deed, without which no good deed is acceptable in Allah's sight, Islam forbids show and ostentation. Show and ostentation is a sign of hypocrisy and an attribute of hypocrites:

> And (likewise) those who spend their wealth (in charity or other good cause) to make a show of it to people (so as to be praised by them) when they believe neither in Allah nor in the Last Day: Whoever has Satan for a comrade, how evil a comrade he is! (4:38)

With its material aspect addressing animal appetites and pleasures, the worldly life is also a play and ostentation. The Qur'an condemns worldly ostentation and boasting of worldly things:

Know that the present, worldly life is but play, vain talk and ostentation, and mutual boasting among you, and competing in wealth and children—it is like when rain comes down and the vegetation grown by it pleases the farmers, (but) then it dries up and you see it turn yellow, then it becomes straw; and in the Hereafter, there is a severe punishment, but also (there is) forgiveness from Allah and His good pleasure (which are everlasting), whereas the present, worldly life is but a transient enjoyment of delusion. (57:20)

Muslims must aim at pleasing Allah or obtaining Allah's good pleasure with whatever worldly benefits or possessions they have:

Made innately appealing to men are passionate love for women, children, (hoarded) treasures of gold and silver, branded horses, cattle, and plantations. Such are enjoyments of the present, worldly life; yet with Allah is the best of the goals to pursue. Say (to them): "Shall I inform you of what is better than those (things that you so passionately seek to obtain)? For those who keep from disobedience to Allah in due reverence for Him and piety there are, with their Lord, Gardens through which rivers flow, wherein they will abide, and spouses purified, and Allah's good pleasure (with them). Allah sees the servants well. (3:14–15)

And hasten, as if competing with one another, to forgiveness from your Lord, and to a Garden as spacious as the heavens and the earth, prepared for the God-revering, pious. (3:133)

UTTERING "IF ALLAH WILLS," BEFORE SAYING ANYTHING ONE INTENDS TO DO

Although human beings are free to make plans for the future and endowed with the necessary equipment to do what they plan, what they will do in the future, even in the present, is not dependent on their willpower exclusively. It is Allah alone Whose absolute Will is dominant over everything that happens including the acts of human beings, and it is His absolute Power Which creates everything and every event including human acts. Without His Will, no one can achieve or bring about anything.

In addition, there are many factors other than human free will that must be taken into consideration in something happening. No one knows whether they will be able to do what they have planned and intended. In fact, no one knows what lies in store even one minute later. Nor does anyone have the absolute power to do whatever they will.

Furthermore, people do not know for sure whether what they intend to do is for their own good. Therefore, we must do what we should according to Allah's Will and commands, taking the necessary measures and making the required preparations, placing our trust in Allah, and then referring to Him whether our intention will be realized or not. Believing that whatever Allah wills is, we must utter "If Allah wills," before saying anything we intend to do in the future. The Qur'an orders as follows:

> And do not say about anything (you intend), "I will do it tomorrow," without (adding), "If Allah wills." And remember and mention Him (straightaway) should you forget (to do so, when expressing an intention for the future). And say: "I hope that my Lord will guide me to what is nearer to right conduct than this (forgetfulness of mine)." (18:23–24)

> "If only you had said, on entering your vineyard, 'Whatever Allah wills (surely has and surely will come to pass); there is no strength (to achieve anything) save with Allah.'" (18:39)

AVOIDING GREED

Islam never approves of greed, or having long-term worldly ambitions. For example, the Qur'an severely criticizes some Jews for their greed as follows:

> And you will undoubtedly find them the greediest of all people for life, more greedy than even those who associate partners with Allah. Every one of them wishes he might be spared for a thousand years, yet his being spared to live will not remove him from the punishment. Allah sees well all that they do. (2:96)

Concerning greed, Said Nursi writes as follows:

> Greed demonstrates its evil consequences throughout the world of animate beings, both at the level of species and at that of particular individuals. On the other hand, seeking one's lawful provision while putting one's trust in Allah is, by contrast, a means to achieving tranquility, and it demonstrates its good effects everywhere. For example, in the animal and human kingdoms only the young, who "demonstrate their trust in Allah through their weakness and helplessness," receive in full measure their rightful and delicious provision from the treasury of the Divine Compassion, Which sets the parents and some other elders at their service; while adult animals that leap greedily at their provision are able to obtain coarse food only at the cost of great effort. It is most pertinent to reflect on the fact that the more powerful wild animals get their food with greater difficulty and at greater intervals than others.
>
> Greed is a source of humiliation and loss. There are so many instances of a greedy person being exposed to loss that the idea that "The greedy are subjected to disappointment and loss," can be found in many proverbs and is a universally accepted truth. That being the case, if we love wealth, we should seek it not with impatience, but with contentment, so that we may earn it abundantly.[148]

Removing Troublesome Things from the Paths of People

In its immaterial sense or with its inner aspect, nature is the collection of Divine laws issuing from His Attributes of Will and Power. With the material aspect of its existence or its materialized form, nature consists of the signs of Allah throughout, and forms a book inscribed by Allah's Names. That is, the Qur'an being the Revealed Book, nature is the Created Book of Allah. Therefore, it has some sort of sacredness. Although nature has been put in the service of humanity, humanity cannot use it however it wishes. For it has some sort of life, and has an integral totality or wholeness: all its parts are interrelated. Without Allah's guidance, humanity cannot use it properly. During the Pilgrimage, Islam forbids cutting green grass and trees. We must be careful not to pollute nature and to protect its purity. As it is forbidden to pollute the environment and throw waste on the roads, removing troublesome things from the paths of people is a meritorious act that Islam encourages.

Allah's Messenger, upon him be peace and blessings, who declared that removing troublesome things from the paths of believers was a branch of faith,[149] said, "A person was going along the path when he found a thorny branch upon it. He pushed it aside and Allah approved (this action) of his and (as a mark of appreciation) granted him pardon."[150]

Abu Barza reported, "I said, 'Allah's Messenger, teach me something so that I may derive benefit from it.' He said, 'Remove troublesome things from the paths of the Muslims.'"[151]

REFRAINING FROM IMPULSIVENESS

The Qur'an frequently refers to a human attribute requiring training or education, and says:

> Yet human (through his actions as well as his words) prays and calls for evil just as he prays and calls for good. Human is prone to be hasty. (17:11)

This attribute of humans arises from their preference for immediate gain and therefore fleeting worldly happiness to the eternal happiness of afterlife, and causes unbelief. The Qur'an frequently warns humankind against this tendency:

> Allah, to Whom belongs whatever is in the heavens and whatever is on the earth; and woe to the unbelievers because of a severe punishment. They choose the present, worldly life in preference to the Hereafter, and bar (people) from Allah's way, and seek to make it appear crooked—those have indeed gone far astray. (14:2–3)

It is a fact that however long they live, everyone is subject to death and will die on a day and in a place unknown to them. In addition, worldly happiness is quite expensive and if the world causes us to laugh one moment, it makes us weep one day. Therefore, we must pursue the eternal happiness of the afterlife to which the Qur'an calls us:

> But you (O humans) are disposed to prefer the life of this world, while the Hereafter is better and more lasting. (87:16–17)

> Made innately appealing to men are passionate love for women, children, (hoarded) treasures of gold and silver, branded horses, cattle, and plantations. Such are enjoyments of the present, worldly life; yet with Allah is the best of the goals to pursue. Say (to them): "Shall I inform you of what is better than those (things that you so passionately seek to obtain)? For those who keep from disobedience to Allah in due reverence for Him and piety there are, with their Lord, Gardens through which rivers flow, wherein they will abide, and spouses purified, and Allah's good pleasure (with them). Allah sees the servants well: Those (the God-revering, pious) pray: "Our Lord, we do indeed believe, so forgive us our sins and guard us against the punishment of the Fire"; Those who are persevering (in misfortune and steadfast in fulfilling Allah's commandments, and in refraining from sins), and truthful (in their words and actions, and true to their covenants), and devoutly obedient, and who spend (out of what Allah has provided for them, in His cause and for the needy), and who implore Allah's forgiveness before daybreak. (3:14–17)

PRAYING FOR ALLAH'S MERCY FOR ONE WHO SNEEZES AND THANKS AND PRAISES ALLAH

Anas ibn Malik, may Allah be pleased with him, narrates:

> Two men sneezed before the Prophet, upon him be peace and blessings. The Prophet said to one of them, "May Allah bestow His mercy on you," but he did not say that to the other. On being asked (why), the Prophet, upon him be peace and blessings, said, "That one praised Allah (at the time of sneezing), while the other did not praise Allah."[152]

Al-Bara', may Allah be pleased with him, narrates:

The Prophet, upon him be peace and blessings, ordered us to do seven (things): He ordered us to pay a visit to the sick; to follow funeral processions; to say, "May Allah bestow His mercy on you!" to one who sneezes if he says, "All praise and thanks be to Allah!"; to accept invitation (to a wedding banquet); to return greetings; to help the oppressed; and to help others to fulfill their oaths (provided it was not sinful).[153]

Abu Hurayra, may Allah be pleased with him, relates:

The Prophet, upon him be peace and blessings, said, "Allah loves sneezing but dislikes yawning; so if anyone of you sneezes and then praises Allah, every Muslim who hears him (praising Allah) has to say "May Allah bestow His mercy on you!" to him. But as regards yawning, it is from Satan, so if one of you yawns, he should try his best to stop it, for when anyone of you yawns, Satan laughs at him."[154]

CHAPTER 4

Verses from the Qur'an and a
Collection of *Hadith*s Concerning
Good, Islamic Morals

VERSES FROM THE QUR'AN AND A COLLECTION OF
*HADITH*S CONCERNING GOOD, ISLAMIC MORALS

VERSES FROM THE QUR'AN

- Your Lord has decreed that you worship none but Him alone, and treat parents with the best of kindness. Should one of them, or both, attain old age in your lifetime, do not say "Ugh!" to them (as an indication of complaint or impatience), nor push them away; and always address them in gracious words. Lower to them the wing of humility out of mercy, and say, "My Lord, have mercy on them even as they cared for me in childhood." Your Lord best knows what is in your souls (in respect of all matters, including what you think of your parents). If you are righteous (in your thoughts and deeds), then surely He is All-Forgiving to those who turn to Him in humble contrition.

- And give his due to the relative, as well as the destitute and the wayfarer.

- And do not squander (your wealth) senselessly. Surely squanderers are ever brothers of satans; and Satan is ever ungrateful to his Lord. But if you (must) turn away from those (who are in need because you are yourself in need, and) seeking mercy from your Lord in hopeful expectation, then (at least) speak to them gently.

- Do not keep your hand bound to your neck (in niggardliness), nor stretch it without any restraint, or else you will be left sitting reproached and denuded. Surely your Lord Allah enlarges provision for whom He wills, and straitens it (for whom He wills). Indeed He is fully aware of His servants and sees them well.

- Do not kill your children for fear of poverty; it is We Who provide for them as well as for you. Killing them is surely a grave sin.
- Do not draw near to any unlawful sexual intercourse; surely it is a shameful, indecent thing, and an evil way (leading to individual and social corruption).
- Do not kill any soul, which Allah has made forbidden, except in just cause. If anyone has been killed wrongfully and intentionally, We have given his heir (as defender of his rights) the authority (to claim retribution or damages or to forgive outright).
- And do not draw near to the property of the orphan except in the best way (such as to improve and increase it) until he comes of age and is strong;
- And fulfill the covenant: the covenant is surely subject to questioning (on the Day of Judgment, you will be held accountable for your covenant).
- Give full measure when you measure, and weigh with a true, accurate balance. That is what is good and (to do so is) best in the long term.
- Do not follow that of which you have no knowledge (whether it is good or bad), and refrain from groundless assertions and conjectures. Surely the hearing, the sight, and the heart—each of these is subject to questioning about it (you are answerable, and will be called to account, for each of these on the Day of Judgment).
- Do not strut about the earth in haughty self-conceit; for you can never split the earth (no matter how hard you stamp your foot), nor can you stretch to the mountains in height (no matter how strenuously you seek to impress). The evil of all this is abhorrent in the sight of your Lord. All this is (part) of the Wisdom which your Lord has revealed to you (O Messenger). (As the source and basis of all wisdom), do not set up with Allah another deity, or you will be cast into Hell, blamed and disowned. (17:23–38)

- Give thanks to Allah. Whoever gives thanks to Allah, gives thanks but for (the good of) his own soul; and whoever is ungrateful, surely Allah is the All-Wealthy and Self-Sufficient (absolutely independent of the whole creation), All-Praiseworthy.

- Do not associate partners with Allah. Surely associating partners with Allah is indeed a tremendous wrong.

- We have enjoined on human in respect with his parents: his mother bore him in strain upon strain, and his weaning was in two years. (So, O human,) be thankful to Me and to your parents. To Me is the final homecoming. But if they strive with you to make you associate with Me something of which you certainly have no knowledge (and which is absolutely contrary to Knowledge), do not obey them. Even then, treat them with kindness and due consideration in respect of (the life of) this world. Follow the way of him who has turned to Me with utmost sincerity and committed himself to seeking My approval. Then (O all human beings), to Me is your return, and then I will make you understand all that you were doing (and call you to account).

- Whether good or evil, if a deed should have the weight of only a mustard-seed, and though it be kept hidden in a rock, in the heavens or in the earth, Allah brings it to light (for judgment). Surely Allah is All-Subtle (penetrating to the most minute dimensions of all things), All-Aware.

- Establish the Prayer in conformity with its conditions, enjoin and promote what is right and good, and forbid and try to prevent the evil, and bear patiently whatever may befall you. Surely (all of) that is among greatly meritorious things requiring great resolution to fulfill.

- Do not turn your face from people in scornful pride, nor move on earth haughtily. Surely Allah does not love anyone proud and boastful.

- Be modest in your bearing, and subdue your voice.

- Do you not see that Allah has made all that is in the heavens and all that is on the earth of service to you, and lavished on you His favors, outward and inward? And yet, among people are those who dispute about Allah without having any true knowledge or any true guidance, or an enlightening Divine Book. When such people are told to follow what Allah has sent down, they say, "No, but we follow that (the traditions, customs, beliefs, and practices) which we found our forefathers in." What! Even if Satan is inviting them to the punishment of the Blaze (by suggesting to them the way of their forefathers)? (The truth is that) whoever submits his whole being to Allah and is devoted to doing good, aware that Allah is seeing him, he has indeed taken hold of the firm, unbreakable handle. With Allah rests the outcome for all matters. (31:12–22)

A SELECTION OF *HADITH*S CONCERNING GOOD, ISLAMIC MORALS

- Refrain from unlawful things and so become a servant of Allah most devoted to Him. Be content with what Allah has assigned for you and so become the riches of humankind. Do good to your neighbor and so become a true believer. Wish for others what you wish for yourself and so become a true Muslim. Do not laugh much, for laughing much kills the heart.[1]
- My Lord enjoined on me the following nine things: that I fear Allah both in the open and in seclusion; that I say what is true and just both in anger and in contentment; that I be economical both in time of plenty and in time of want; that I continue my relationship with those who have severed their relationship with me; that I continue giving to those who leave me deprived; that I forgive those who oppress me; that my silence be reflective thought; that my speech be remembrance of Allah; that my look be for learning lessons; and that I enjoin and encourage what is good.[2]

- There are two virtues that whoever has them Allah records him among those who are thankful and patient: to consider those who are superior to him in devotion to the Religion and follow them; and to consider those who are inferior to him in having worldly things and thank to and praise Allah because of the superiority He has granted him.[3]

- Uqba ibn Amir asked Allah's Messenger, "How will we able to be saved (from Allah's punishment)?" The Messenger replied, "Hold your tongue; entertain as many guests as possible; and weep for your sins."[4]

- The Fire has been forbidden for the one who is near to people, mild and lenient, and who show people to the easy way (of doing things).[5]

- Let no one among you say, "I am like everyone else. If they do me good, I will do them good; but if they do me an evil, I will also do them an evil." Rather, control yourselves, and if people do you good, you also do good; if they do you an evil, do not attempt to do them an evil.[6]

- Let him be humbled unto dust whose sins are not forgiven although he has reached and left behind the month of Ramadan; let him be humbled unto dust who accompanies either of his parents during their old age or he accompanies both of them, but he cannot enter Paradise; let him be humbled unto dust who does not invoke Allah's blessing and peace upon me although I am mentioned beside him.[7]

BELIEVERS PRAISED IN THE QUR'AN

- Those who believe in the Unseen, establish the Prayer in conformity with its conditions, and out of what We have provided for them (of wealth, knowledge, power, etc.,), they spend (to provide sustenance for the needy and in Allah's cause, purely for the good pleasure of Allah and without placing others under obligation). And those who believe in what is sent down to you, and what was sent down before you (such as the Torah, Gospel and Psalms, and the Scrolls of Abraham), and in the Hereafter, they have certainty of faith. Those (illustrious ones) stand on true guidance (originating in the Qur'an) from their Lord; and they are those who are the prosperous. (2:3–5)

- Those (the God-revering, pious) pray, "Our Lord, we do indeed believe, so forgive us our sins and guard us against the punishment of the Fire"; Those who are persevering (in misfortune and steadfast in fulfilling Allah's commandments, and in refraining from sins), and truthful (in their words and actions, and true to their covenants), and devoutly obedient, and who spend (out of what Allah has provided for them, in His way and for the needy), and who implore Allah's forgiveness before daybreak. (3:16–17)

- And hasten, as if competing with one another, to forgiveness from your Lord, and to a Garden as spacious as the heavens and the earth, prepared for the God-revering, pious. They spend (out of what Allah has provided for them,) both in ease and hardship, ever-restraining their rage (even when provoked and able to retaliate), and pardoning people (their offenses). Allah loves (such) people who are devoted to doing good, aware that Allah is seeing them. They are also the ones who, when they have committed a shameful deed or wronged themselves (through any kind of sinful act), immediately remember Allah and implore Him to forgive their sins—for who will forgive sins save Allah?—and do not persist knowingly in whatever (evil) they have committed. Such are the ones whose reward is forgiveness from their Lord and Gardens through which rivers flow, to abide therein. How excellent is the reward of those who always do good deeds! (3:135–136)

- O you who believe! Whoever of you turns away from his Religion, (know that) in time, Allah will raise up a people whom He loves, and who love Him, most humble towards the believers, dignified and commanding in the face of the unbelievers, striving (continuously and in solidarity) in Allah's cause, and fearing not the censure of any who censure. That is Allah's grace and bounty, which He grants to whom He wills. Allah is All-Embracing (with His profound grace), All-Knowing. (5:54)

- The true believers are only those who, when Allah is mentioned, their hearts tremble with awe, and when His Revelations are recited to them, it strengthens them in faith, and they put their trust in their Lord. They establish the Prayer in conformity with its conditions, and out of whatever We have provided for them (of wealth, knowledge, power, etc.), they spend (to provide sustenance for the needy, and in Allah's cause, purely for the good pleasure of Allah, and without placing others under obligation.) Those (illustrious ones) are they who are truly believers. For them are ranks with their Lord (to be granted one after the other), and forgiveness (to bring unforeseen blessings), and generous, honorable provisions. Those who have believed and emigrated (to the home of Islam) and striven (with their wealth and persons) in Allah's cause, and those who give refuge (to them) and help (them) – those (illustrious ones) are the believers in truth. For them is forgiveness (to bring unforeseen blessings) and honorable, generous provision. (8:2–4, 74)

- The first and foremost (to embrace Islam and excel others in virtue) among the Emigrants and the Helpers, and those who follow them in devotion to doing good, aware that Allah is seeing them—Allah is well-pleased with them, and they are well-pleased with Him, and He has prepared for them Gardens throughout which rivers flow, therein to abide forever. That is the supreme triumph. (9:100)

- Those who return in repentance to Allah, and those who worship Allah, and those who praise Allah, and those who travel (with such aims as conveying Allah's Message, or studying and making investigations for Allah's sake or reflecting on Allah's signs), and those who bow down in awe of Allah, and those who prostrate themselves before Allah in submission, and those who enjoin and promote what is right and good, and forbid and try to prevent evil, and those who keep to the bounds set by Allah: give glad tidings to the believers. (9:112)

- Those who fulfill Allah's covenant (responsible for the order in the universe, and able to establish the peace, order and harmony in human life) and do not break the pledge (that they shall worship none save Allah, and fulfill all the moral, spiritual, and social obligations resulting from believing in and worshipping only One Allah); and those who unite the bonds Allah has commanded to be joined (among kin as a requirement of blood relationship, and among people as required by human social interdependence), and stand in awe of their Lord, and fearful of (facing) the most evil reckoning; and those who endure patiently (all adversities they face in Allah's cause) in pursuit of where Allah's good, eternal pleasure lies, and they establish the Prayer in conformity with its conditions, and spend of whatever We provide for them secretly and openly, and repel the evil with good. Such are those for whom there is the ultimate (everlasting) abode. (13:20–22)

- Prosperous indeed are the believers. They are in their Prayer humble and fully submissive (being overwhelmed by the awe and majesty of Allah). They always turn away from and avoid whatever is vain and frivolous. They are in a constant effort to give alms and purify their own selves and wealth. They strictly guard their private parts, and their chastity and modesty. They are faithful and true to their trusts (which either Allah, society, or an individual places in their charge), and to their pledges (between them and Allah or other persons or society). They are ever mindful guardians of their Prayers (including all the rites of which they are constituted). Those (illustrious ones) are the inheritors, who will inherit the highest floor of Paradise. Therein they will abide forever. (23:1–5, 8–11)

- While as for those who live in awe because of deep reverence for their Lord, who have renewed, ever-strengthening faith in their Lord's signs and Revelations, who never associate partners with their Lord, who do whatever they do, and give whatever they give, in charity and for Allah's cause, with their hearts trembling at the thought that they are bound to turn to their Lord (remaining anxious, for they are unsure whether Allah will accept their deeds from them and be pleased with them)— it is those (illustrious ones) who hasten to do all kinds of virtuous deeds, and they are in a virtuous competition with one another in doing them. (23:57–61)

- The (true) servants of the All-Merciful are they who move on the earth gently and humbly, and when the ignorant, foolish ones address them (with insolence or vulgarity, as befits their ignorance and foolishness), they respond with (words of) peace (without engaging in hostility with them); and (those true servants of the All-Merciful are they) who spend (some of) the night (in worship) prostrating before their Lord and standing;

and who entreat (whether after the Prayers or at other times), "Our Lord! Ward off from us the punishment of Hell; its punishment is surely constant anguish: How evil indeed it is as a final station and permanent abode!"; and who, when they spend (both for their own and others' needs), are neither wasteful nor niggardly, and (are aware that) there is a happy mean between those (two extremes); and who invoke no other deity along with Allah, and do not kill any soul—which Allah has made forbidden—except by right (for just cause and after due process), and do not commit unlawful sexual intercourse. And (those true servants of the All-Merciful are they) who do not take part in, or bear witness to, any vanity or falsehood (and who will not deem anything true unless they know it to be so for certain), and when they happen to pass by anything vain and useless, pass by it with dignity; and who, when they are reminded of the Revelations of their Lord (and His signs in the creation as well as in their inner world, as a basis of advice or teaching or discussion), do not remain unmoved as though deaf and blind; and who say, "Our Lord! Grant us that our spouses and offspring may be a means of happiness for us, and enable us to lead others in piety (to become a means of the promotion of piety and virtue)." Such (illustrious) ones will be rewarded with the loftiest mansion (in Paradise) for their steadfastness (in their obedience to Allah and in their cause in spite of all adversities and persecutions), and they will be met therein with a greeting of welcome and peace, therein to abide. How good it is as a final station and permanent abode. (25:63–76)

- When it is recited to them, they say, "We believe in it. Surely it is the truth from our Lord. Even before this, We were such as submitted (to the Divine Will)." These will be granted their reward twice over because they have remained steadfast (in following their religion, free of falsehood, and so keeping themselves above all prejudices to believe in and follow the Qur'an and Muhammad); and they repel evil with good, and out of what We have provided for them (of wealth, knowledge, power, etc.), they spend (in Allah's cause and for the needy, and purely for the good pleasure of Allah). When they hear any vain (useless or aggressive) talk, they turn away from it, without reciprocating it, and say (to those who are engaged in it), "To us are accounted our deeds, and to you, your deeds. Peace be upon you! We do not seek to mix with the ignorant (those unaware of Allah, true guidance and right and wrong)." (28:53–55)

- Only they (truly) believe in Our signs and Revelations who, when they are mentioned of them (by way of advice and instruction), fall down in prostration, and glorify their Lord with His praise, and they do not behave with haughtiness. Their sides forsake their beds at night, calling out to their Lord in fear (of His punishment) and hope (for His forgiveness, grace, and good pleasure), and out of what We have provided for them (of wealth, knowledge, power, etc.), they spend (to provide sustenance for the needy and in Allah's cause, purely for the good pleasure of Allah and without placing others under obligation). (32:15–16)

- Surely all men and women who submit to Allah (whose submission is attested by their words and deeds), and all truly believing men and truly believing women, and all devoutly obedient men and devoutly obedient women, and all men and women honest and truthful in their speech (and true to their words in their actions), and all men and women who persevere (in obedience to Allah through all adversity), and all men and women humble (in mind and heart before Allah), and all men and women who give in alms (and in Allah's cause), and all men and women who fast (as an obligatory or commended act of devotion), and all men and women who guard their chastity (and avoid exposing their private parts), and all men and women who remember and mention Allah much—for them (all),

Allah has prepared forgiveness (to bring unforeseen blessings) and a tremendous reward. (33:35)

- Those who avoid the major sins and indecent, shameful deeds (which are indeed to be counted among major sins), and when they become angry, even then they forgive (rather than retaliate in kind); and those who answer the call of their Lord and obey Him (in His orders and prohibitions), and establish the Prayer in conformity with its conditions; and whose affairs are by consultation among themselves; and who spend out of what We provide for them (to provide sustenance for the needy, and in Allah's cause); and those who, when an unjust aggression is inflicted on (any or all of) them, defend themselves and one another (to end the aggression). (42:37–39)

مُحَمَّدٌ رَسُولُ اللهِ وَالَّذِينَ مَعَهُ أَشِدَّاءُ عَلَى الْكُفَّارِ رُحَمَاءُ بَيْنَهُمْ تَرَاهُمْ رُكَّعًا سُجَّدًا يَبْتَغُونَ فَضْلًا مِنَ اللهِ وَرِضْوَانًا سِيمَاهُمْ فِي وُجُوهِهِمْ مِنْ أَثَرِ السُّجُودِ ذٰلِكَ مَثَلُهُمْ فِي التَّوْرَاةِ وَمَثَلُهُمْ فِي الْإِنْجِيلِ كَزَرْعٍ أَخْرَجَ شَطْأَهُ فَآزَرَهُ فَاسْتَغْلَظَ فَاسْتَوَى عَلَى سُوقِهِ يُعْجِبُ الزُّرَّاعَ لِيَغِيظَ بِهِمُ الْكُفَّارَ وَعَدَ اللهُ الَّذِينَ آمَنُوا وَعَمِلُوا الصَّالِحَاتِ مِنْهُمْ مَغْفِرَةً وَأَجْرًا عَظِيمًا

- Muhammad is the Messenger of Allah; and those who are in his company are firm and unyielding against the unbelievers, and compassionate among themselves. You see them (constant in the Prayer) bowing down and prostrating, seeking favor with Allah and His approval and good pleasure. Their marks are on their faces, traced by prostration. This is their description in the Torah; and their description in the Gospel: like a seed that has sprouted its shoot, then it has strengthened it, and then risen firmly on its stem, delighting the sowers (with joy and wonder), that through them He fills the unbelievers with rage. Allah has promised all those among them who believe and do good, righteous deeds forgiveness (to bring unforeseen blings) and a tremendous reward. (48:29)

CHAPTER 5

The Unequalled Character of Allah's
Messenger

THE UNEQUALLED CHARACTER OF
ALLAH'S MESSENGER

Allah's Messenger, upon him be peace and blessings, says, "I have been sent to perfect the standards and beauties of good morals."[1] Thus perfection (i.e., perfected morality or character) is the fruit and evidence of Islamic teachings and life, and signifies that one is moving from the status of being a potential human being to that of being a true human being. For this reason, both the Qur'an and the Messenger attach great importance to morality.

When asked about the Messenger's morality or character, his wife 'A'isha answered that it was the Qur'an.[2] In other words, the Messenger embodied the Qur'an or, as some have described, was a moving or walking Qur'an. So, we will also examine Islamic morality in the Messenger's virtues as described in *Muhammad: The Messenger of Allah – An Analysis of the Prophet's Life*, by M. Fethullah Gülen.[3]

THE PROPHET OF UNIVERSAL MERCY

The beginning of existence was an act of mercy and compassion without which the universe would be in chaos. Everything came into existence through compassion, and by compassion it continues to exist in harmony. Muslim sages say that the universe is the All-Compassionate One's breath. In other words, the universe was created to manifest the Divine Name the All-Compassionate. Its subsistence depends upon the same Name. This Name manifests itself first as the All-Provider, so that all living creatures can receive the food or nourishment they need to survive.

Life is Allah Almighty's foremost and most manifest blessing, and the true and everlasting life is that of the Hereafter. Since we can deserve that life by pleasing Allah, He sent Prophets and revealed Scriptures out of His compassion for humanity. For this reason, while mentioning His blessings upon humanity in *Surat ar-Rahman* (the All-Merciful), He begins, *Ar-Rahman. He has taught the Qur'an, He has created man; He has taught him speech* (55:1–4).

All aspects of this life are a rehearsal for the afterlife, and every creature is engaged in action toward this end. Order is evident in every effort, and compassion resides in every achievement. Some "natural" events or social convulsions may seem disagreeable at first, but we should not regard them as incompatible with compassion. They are like dark clouds or lightning and thunder that, although frightening, nevertheless bring us good tidings of rain. Thus the whole universe praises the All-Compassionate.

Prophet Muhammad, upon him be peace and blessings, is like a spring of pure water in the heart of a desert, a source of light in an all-enveloping darkness. Whoever appeals to this spring can take as much water as needed to quench their thirst, to become purified of all their sins, and to become illumined with the light of belief. Mercy was like a magic key in his hands, for with it he opened hearts that were so hardened and rusty that no one thought they could be opened. But he did even more: he lit a torch of belief in them.

The Messenger preached Islam, the religion of universal mercy. His compassion encompassed every creature. He desired, of course, that everyone be guided. In fact, this was his greatest concern: *Yet it may be, if they believe not in this Message, you will consume yourself, following after them, with grief* (18:6). But how should he deal with those who persisted in unbelief and fought him to destroy both him and his Message? He had to fight such people. But when they wounded him severely at Uhud, he raised his hands and prayed, "O Allah, forgive my people, for they do not know."[4]

The Meccans, his own people, inflicted so much suffering on him that he finally emigrated to Medina. Even after that, the next five years were far from peaceful. However, when he conquered Mecca without bloodshed in the twenty-first year of his Prophethood, he asked the Meccan unbelievers, "How do you expect me to treat you?" They responded unanimously, "You are a noble one, the son of a noble one." He then told them his decision, "You may leave, for no reproach this day shall be on you. May Allah forgive you. He is the Most Compassionate of the Compassionate."[5] Sultan Mehmed the Conqueror said the same thing to the defeated Byzantines after conquering Istanbul 825 years later. Such is the universal compassion of Islam.

The Messenger displayed the highest degree of compassion toward the believers:

$$ لَقَدْ جَاءَكُمْ رَسُولٌ مِنْ أَنْفُسِكُمْ عَزِيزٌ عَلَيْهِ مَا عَنِتُّمْ حَرِيصٌ عَلَيْكُمْ بِالْمُؤْمِنِينَ رَءُوفٌ رَحِيمٌ $$

There has come to you (O people) a Messenger from among yourselves; extremely grievous to him is your suffering; full of concern for you is he, and for the believers, full of pity and compassion. (9:128)

He lowered unto believers his wing of tenderness through mercy (15:88), and was the guardian of believers and nearer to them than their selves (33:6). When a Companion died, he asked those at the funeral if the deceased had left any debts. On learning that he had, the Prophet mentioned the above verse and announced that the creditors should come to him for repayment.[6]

Allah did not send a collective destruction upon the unbelievers during his time, although He had eradicated many such people in the past: *But Allah would not punish them so long as you were among them; and Allah is not to punish them (or other people) while they implore Him for forgiveness for their sins* (8:33). This verse refers to unbelievers of any time. Allah will not destroy peoples altogether as long as those who follow the Messenger are alive. Besides, He has left the door of repentance open until the Last Day. Anyone can accept Islam or ask Allah's forgiveness, regardless of how sinful they consider themselves to be.

For this reason, a Muslim's enmity toward unbelievers is a form of pity. When 'Umar saw an eighty-year-old man, he sat down and sobbed. When asked why he did so, he replied, "Allah assigned him so long a life span, but he has not been able to find the true path." 'Umar was a disciple of the Messenger, who said, "I was not sent to call down curses upon people, but as a mercy."[7] and "I am Muhammad, and Ahmad (praised one), al-Muqaffi (the Last Prophet); I am al-Hashir (the final Prophet in whose presence the dead will be resurrected); the Prophet of repentance (the Prophet for whom the door of repentance will always remain open), and the Prophet of mercy."[8] When Ma'iz was punished for fornication, a Companion verbally abused him. The Messenger frowned at him and said, "You have backbitten your friend. His repentance and asking Allah's pardon for his sin would be enough to forgive all the sinners in the world."[9]

The Messenger was particularly compassionate toward children. Whenever he saw a child crying, he sat beside him or her and shared his or her feelings. He felt a mother's pain for her child more than the mother herself. Once he said, "I stand in prayer and wish to prolong it. However, I hear a child cry and shorten the prayer to lessen the mother's anxiety."[10]

He took children in his arms and hugged them. Once when the Messenger was hugging his beloved grandsons Hasan and Husayn, al-Aqra' ibn Habis told him, "I have ten children, and I have never kissed any one of them." The Messenger responded, "One who is not merciful to others is not treated mercifully. What can I do for you if Allah has removed mercy from you?"[11] He said, "Pity those on the earth so that those in the heavens will pity you."[12] When Sa'd ibn 'Ubada became ill, the Messenger visited him at home and, seeing his faithful Companion in a pitiful state, began to cry. He said, "Allah does not punish because of tears or grief, but He punishes because of this," and he pointed to his tongue.[13]

A member of the Banu Muqarrin clan once beat his maidservant. She informed the Messenger, who sent for the master. He said, "You have beaten her without any justifiable right. Free her."[14] Freeing a slave was far better for the master than being punished in the Hereafter because of that act. The Messenger always protected and supported widows, orphans, the poor and disabled even before announcing his Prophethood. When he returned home in excitement from the Hira Cave on Mount Nur after the first Revelation, his wife Khadija told him, "Allah will never disgrace you. You keep good relations with your kith and kin, help the poor and the destitute, serve your guests generously, and assist the deserving calamity-afflicted ones."[15]

His compassion encompassed animals. He said, "Allah guided a prostitute to truth and ultimately to Paradise because she gave water to a dog dying of thirst. Another woman was sent to Hell because she left a cat to die of hunger."[16] While returning from a battle, a few Companions removed some young birds from their nest to stroke them. The mother bird came back and, not finding its babies, began to fly around screeching. When told of this, the Messenger became angry and ordered the birds to be put back in the nest.[17] Ibn 'Abbas reported that when the Messenger saw a man sharpening his knife directly before the sheep to be slaughtered, he asked, "Do you want to kill it many times?"[18]

The Messenger lived for others, and was a mercy for all the worlds, a manifestation of Compassion.

HIS MILDNESS AND FORBEARANCE

Mildness is another dimension of the Messenger's character. He was a bright mirror in which Allah reflected His Mercy. Mildness is a reflection of compassion. Allah made His Messenger mild and gentle, thereby allowing him to gain many converts to Islam and overcome numerous obstacles.

After the victory of Badr, the Battle of Uhud was a severe trial for the young Muslim community. Although the Messenger wanted to fight on the outskirts of Medina, most Muslims desired to fight on an open battlefield. When the two armies met at the foot of Mount Uhud, the Messenger, upon him be peace and blessings, positioned fifty archers in ʿAynayn pass and ordered them not to move without his permission, even if they saw that the Muslims had won a decisive victory.

The Muslim army, having only one-third of the men and equipment of the enemy, almost defeated the Meccan polytheists in the initial stage. Seeing the enemy fleeing, these archers forgot the Prophet's command and left their post. Khalid ibn Walid, the Meccan cavalry's commander, saw this and, riding round the mountain, attacked the Muslims from behind. The fleeing enemy soldiers turned back and caught the Muslims in crossfire. They began to lose, more than seventy were martyred, and the Messenger was wounded.

He might have reproached those who had urged him to pursue their desires as well as the archers who had abandoned their post, but he did not. Instead, he showed leniency,

> It was by a mercy from Allah that (at the time of the setback), you (O Messenger) were lenient with them (your Companions). Had you been harsh and hard-hearted, they would surely have scattered away from about you. Then pardon them, pray for their forgiveness, and take counsel with them in the affairs (of public concern); and when you are resolved (on a course of action), put your trust in Allah. Surely Allah loves those who put their trust (in Him). (3:159)

This verse shows two prerequisites for leadership: mildness and leniency toward those who make well-intentioned mistakes, and the importance of consultation in public administration.

This mildness and forgiveness was a reflection of Allah's Names the All-Mild, All-Clement, and All-Forgiving. Allah does not stop providing for people despite their rebellion or unbelief. While most people disobey Him by indulging in unbelief, by explicitly or implicitly associating partners with Him, or transgressing His Commands, the sun continues to send them its heat and light, clouds full of rain come to their aid, and the soil never stops feeding them with its fruits and plants. Allah's Clemency and Forgiveness are reflected through the Messenger's compassion, mildness, and forgiveness.

Allah's Messenger, upon him be peace and blessings, was never angry with anybody because of what they did to him. When his wife 'A'isha was slandered, he did not consider punishing the slanderers even after she was cleared by the Qur'an. Bedouins often behaved impolitely with him, but he did not even frown at them. Although extremely sensitive, he always showed forbearance toward both friend and foe.

For example, while he was distributing the spoils of war after the Battle of Hunayn, Dhu al-Huwaysira objected, "Be just, O Muhammad." This was an unforgivable insult, for the Prophet had been sent to establish justice. Unable to endure such offences, 'Umar demanded permission to kill "that hypocrite" on the spot. But the Messenger only replied, "Who else will show justice if I am not just? If I don't show justice, then I am lost and brought to naught."[19]

Once when the Prophet was going home after talking to his Companions in the mosque, a Bedouin pulled him by the collar and said rudely, "O Muhammad! Give me my due! Load up my two camels! For you will load them up with neither your own wealth nor that of your father!" Without showing any sign of being offended, he told others, "Give him what he wants!"[20]

Zayd ibn San'an, may Allah be pleased with him, narrates:

> Before I embraced Islam, the Messenger borrowed some money from me. I went to him to collect my debt before its due time, and insulted him, "O you children of 'Abd al-Muttalib, you are very reluctant to pay your debts!" 'Umar became very angry with me and shouted, "O enemy of Allah! Were it not for the treaty between us and the Jewish community, I would cut off your head! Speak to the Messenger politely!" However, the Messenger smiled at me and, turning to 'Umar, said, "Pay him,

and add twenty gallons (of dates) to it, because you frightened him."

'Umar, may Allah be pleased with him, relates the rest of the story:

> We went together. On the way, Zayd said unexpectedly, "O 'Umar, you were angry with me. But I find in him all the features of the Last Prophet recorded in the Torah, the Old Testament. It contains this verse: *His mildness surpasses his anger. The severity of impudence to him increases him only in mildness and forbearance.* To test his forbearance, I provoked him deliberately. Now I am convinced that he is the Prophet whose coming the Torah predicted. So, I believe and bear witness that he is the Last Prophet." [21]

This mildness and forbearance was enough for the conversion of Zayd ibn San'an, a Jewish scholar.

The Messenger's mildness and forbearance captured hearts and preserved Muslim unity. As stated in the Qur'an (3:159), if he had been harsh and hard-hearted, people would have abandoned him. But those who saw him and listened to him were so endowed with Divine manifestations that they became saints. For example, Khalid ibn Walid was the Qurayshi general who caused the Muslims to experience a reverse at Uhud. However, when he was not included in the army that set out on the day after his conversion, he was so upset that he wept.

Like Khalid, Ikrima and 'Amr ibn al-'As were among those who did great harm to the Messenger and the Muslims. After their conversions, each became a sword of Islam drawn against wrongdoing unbelievers. Ibn Hisham, Abu Jahl's brother, converted to Islam shortly before the Messenger passed away. He was such a sincere Muslim that just before he was martyred at Yarmuk, he did not drink the water that Hudayfa al-'Adawi offered him. Rather, he asked that it be given to nearby wounded fellow Muslim groaning for water. He died, having preferred a fellow Muslim over himself.[22]

The Messenger, upon him be peace and blessings, brought up the Companions. Their greatness is shown in the fact that despite their small numbers, they successfully conveyed Islam to the furthest reaches of Asia and Africa within a few decades. In those areas, Islam became so deeply rooted that despite the concerted efforts by the superpowers of each era to extinguish Islam, it continues to gain new momentum and represents the only realistic alternative for human salvation. The Companions were transformed from their wretched pre-Islamic state to being guides and teachers of a considerable part of humanity until the Last Day, the vanguard of the most magnificent civilization in history.

In addition, the Messenger was absolutely balanced. His universal compassion did not prevent him from executing Divine justice, and his mildness and forbearance kept him from breaching any Islamic rule or humiliating himself. For example, during a military campaign Usama ibn Zayd threw an enemy soldier to the ground. When he was about to kill him, the man declared his belief in Islam. Judging this to be the result of a fear of imminent death, Usama killed him. When told of the incident, the Messenger reprimanded Usama severely, "Did you cleave his heart open and see (if what you suspected is true)?" He repeated this so many times that Usama said later, "I wished I had not yet become a Muslim on the day I was scolded so severely."[23]

Likewise, once Abu Dharr got so angry with Bilal that he insulted him: "You son of a black woman!" Bilal came to the Messenger and reported the incident in tears. The Messenger reproached Abu Dharr: "Do you still have a sign of *Jahiliya*?" Full of repentance, Abu Dharr lay on the ground and said, "I won't raise my head (meaning he wouldn't get up) unless Bilal put his foot on it to pass over it." Bilal forgave him, and they were reconciled.[24] Such was the brotherhood and humanity Islam created between once-savage people.

His Generosity

Allah's Messenger, upon him be peace and blessings, is the most polished mirror in which Allah's Names and Attributes are reflected to the highest degree. As the perfect manifestation of these Names and Attributes, an embodiment of the Qur'an and Islam, he is the greatest and most decisive and comprehensive proof of Allah's Existence and Unity, and of the truth of Islam and the Qur'an. Those who saw him remembered Allah automatically. Each of his virtues reflected a Name or Attribute of Allah, and is a proof of his Prophethood. Like his mildness and forbearance, his generosity is another dimension of his excellent, matchless personality, a reflection and proof of his Prophethood.

The people of Arabia were renowned for their generosity even in pre-Islamic times. When we look at that era's poetry, we see that the Arabs were proud of their generosity. However, their generosity was not for the sake of Allah or for an altruistic motive; rather, it was the cause of self-pride. But the Messenger's generosity was purely for Allah's sake. He never mentioned it, and did not like to have it mentioned. When a poet praised him for his generosity, he attributed whatever good he had or did to Allah. He never attributed his virtues and good deeds to himself.

The Messenger liked to distribute whatever he had. He engaged in trade until his Prophethood, and had considerable wealth. Afterwards, he and his wealthy wife Khadija spent everything in the way of Allah. When Khadija died, there was no money for her burial shroud. The Messenger had to borrow money to bury his own wife, the first person to embrace Islam and its first supporter.[25]

If the Messenger had desired, he could have been the richest man in Mecca. But he rejected such offers without a second thought. Although Allah mandated that one-fifth of all war spoils should be at the Messenger's free disposal, he never spent it on himself or his family. He and his family lived austerely and survived on scanty provisions, for he always gave preference to others.

The Messenger regarded himself as a traveler in this world. Once he said, "What connection do I have with this world? I am like a traveler who takes shade under a tree and then continues on his way."[26] According to him, the world is like a tree under which people are shaded. No one can live forever, so people must prepare here for the second part of the journey, which will end either in Paradise or Hell.

The Messenger, upon him be peace and blessings, was sent to guide people to truth, and so spent his life and possessions to this end. Once 'Umar saw him lying on a rough mat and wept. When the Messenger asked him why he was weeping, 'Umar replied, "O Messenger of Allah, while kings sleep in soft feather beds, you lie on a rough mat. You are the Messenger of Allah, and as such deserve an easy life more than anyone else." He answered, "Don't you agree that the luxuries of the world should be theirs, and that those of the Hereafter should be ours?"[27]

The Messenger, upon him be peace and blessings, was, in the words of al-Bara', "the most handsome person";[28] and in the words of Anas ibn Malik, "the most generous and courageous of people, and the best of them in disposition and behavior."[29] Jabir ibn Samura reports, "Once we were sitting in the mosque, and a full moon was shining above us. The Messenger entered. I looked first at the moon and then at his face. I swear by Allah that his face was brighter than the moon."[30]

The Messenger, upon him be peace and blessings, never refused anyone and, as Farazdak said, only said "No!" when reciting the profession of faith while praying. Once, a Bedouin came and asked the Messenger for something. The Messenger complied with his request. The Bedouin continued to ask, and the Messenger continued to give until he had nothing left. When the Bedouin asked again, he promised that he would give it to him when he had it. Angered by such rudeness, 'Umar said to the Messenger, "You were asked and you gave. Again you were asked and you gave, until you were asked once more and you promised!" 'Umar meant that the Messenger should not make things so difficult for himself. The Messenger did not approve of 'Umar's words. 'Abdullah ibn Hudafa as-Sahmi stood up and said, "O Messenger, give without fear that the Owner of the Seat of Honor will make you poor!" Pleased with such words, the Messenger declared, "I was commanded to do so."[31]

He never refused a request, for it was he who said, "The generous are near to Allah, Paradise, and people, but distant from the Fire. The miserly are distant from Allah, Paradise, and people, but near to the Fire";[32] and, "O people! Surely Allah has chosen for you Islam as religion. Improve your practice of it through generosity and good manners."[33]

HIS MODESTY AND HUMILITY

In society, each person has a window (status) through which he or she looks out to see others and be seen. If the window is built higher than their real stature, people try to make themselves appear taller through vanity and assumed airs. If the window is set lower than their real stature, they must bow in humility in order to look out, see, and be seen. Humility is the measure of one's greatness, just as vanity or conceit is the measure of low character.[34]

The Messenger had a stature so high that it could be said to touch the "roof of the heavens." Therefore, he had no need to be seen. Whoever travels in the realm of virtues sees him before every created being, including angels. Since he is the greatest of humanity, he is the greatest in modesty. This follows the well-known adage, "The greater one is, the more modest one is."

He never regarded himself as greater than anybody else. Only his radiant face and attractive person distinguished him from his Companions. He lived and dressed like the poorest people and sat and ate with them, just as he did with slaves and servants. Once a woman saw him eating and remarked, "He eats like a slave." The Messenger replied, "Could there be a better slave than me? I am a slave of Allah."[35]

One time when he was serving his friends, a Bedouin came in and shouted, "Who is the master of this people?" The Messenger answered in such a way that he introduced himself while expressing a substantial principle of Islamic leadership and public administration: "The people's master is the one who serves them." Ali says that among people the Messenger was one of them. While the Muslims were building their mosque in Medina, the Prophet carried bricks with them.[36]

While digging the trench to defend Medina, the Companions bound a stone around their stomachs to quell their hunger; the Messenger bound two.[37] When a man seeing him for the first time began trembling out of fear, because he found the Prophet's appearance so awe-inspiring, the Messenger calmed him: "Brother, don't be afraid. I am a man, like you, whose mother used to eat dry bread."[38] Allah's Messenger, upon him be peace and blessings, used to run to the aid of everyone, and did not refrain from even being led by an insane woman to help her. It happened several times that an old she-slave who was probably insane pulled him by the hand to help her with her housework, and he complied with her request.[39] 'A'isha reported that the Messenger patched his clothes, repaired his shoes, and helped his wives with the housework.[40]

Although his modesty elevated him to the highest rank, he saw himself as an ordinary servant of Allah: "No one enters Paradise because of his or her deeds." When asked if this was true for him as well, he said that he could enter Paradise only through the Mercy of Allah.[41] Humility is the most important aspect of the Messenger's servanthood. He declared, "Allah exalts the humble and abases the haughty."[42] 'Ali describes the Messenger as follows:

> He was the most generous person in giving, and the mildest and the foremost in patience and perseverance. He was the most truthful in speech, the most amiable and congenial in companionship, and the noblest of them in family. Whoever sees him first is stricken by awe, but whoever knows him closely is deeply attracted to him. Whoever attempts to describe him says, "I have never seen the like of him."[43]

NOTES

_____

CHAPTER 1: ISLAMIC MORALITY

1   *al-Muwatta'*, "Husn al-Khulq" 8; *al-Bukhari*, *Adab al-Mufrad*, HN:273.
2   *al-Bukhari*, "Adab" 39; *Abu Dawud*, "Sunna" 15; *at-Tirmidhi*, "Rada" 11.
3   *al-Bukhari*, "Adab" 39.
4   *Muslim*, "Salah" 110.
5   *at-Tirmidhi*, "Birr" 41.
6   *at-Tirmidhi*, "Birr" 62; *Abu Dawud*, "Adab" 8.
7   *Abu Dawud*, "Adab" 9.
8   Summarized from M. Fethullah Gülen, *Key Concepts in the Practice of Sufism: Emerald Hills of the Heart* (Trans.) The Light, NJ, 2004, Vol., 1, pp., 72–75.
9   Sarraj, Abu Nasr 'Abdullah ibn 'Ali at-Tusi, (d. 959/60 or 988), was one of the famous spiritual guides and scholars. (Trans.)
10 M. Fethullah Gülen, *Key Concepts in the Practice of Sufism: Emerald Hills of the Heart* (Trans.) The Light, NJ, 2004, Vol., 2, pp., 13–16.
11 *al-Bukhari*, "Adab" 86.
12 *Muslim*, "Qadar" 8.
13 *Abu Dawud*, "Sunna" 15; *at-Tirmidhi*, "Rada" 11.
14 *Abu Dawud*, "Adab" 397.
15 *al-Bukhari*, "Adab" 40.
16 *Muslim*, "Birr" 1.
17 *at-Tirmidhi*, "Birr" 3.
18 *at-Tirmidhi*, "Birr" 3.
19 *Abu Dawud*, "Adab" 368.
20 *al-Bukhari*, "Adab" 4.
21 *Abu Dawud*, "Adab" 386.
22 *Abu Dawud*, "Adab" 443.
23 *Abu Dawud*, "Adab" 373; *Muslim*, "Birr" 44.
24 Partly summarized and edited from al-Qaradawi's *The Lawful and Prohibited in Islam*, trans. Muhammad Siddiqi (ASIN:1999).
25 *an-Nasa'i*, "Tahrim," 1:2.
26 *al-Bukhari*, "Adab" 43.
27 *Abu Dawud*, "Adab" 201.
28 *Abu Dawud*, "Adab" 104.
29 *Abu Dawud*, "Adab" 105.

30 *Abu Dawud*, "Adab" 108.

31 *Abu Dawud*, "Adab" 107.

32 *Muslim*, "Birr" 19.

33 *Abu Dawud*, "Adab" 118.

34 *Abu Dawud*, "Adab" 111.

35 *Abu Dawud*, "Adab" 135.

36 *Abu Dawud*, "Adab" 127.

37 *Abu Dawud*, "Adab" 351.

38 *al-Bukhari*, "Adab" 42.

39 *Abu Dawud*, "Adab" 437.

40 *Abu Dawud*, "Adab" 438.

41 *al-Bukhari*, "Isti'dhan" 27.

42 *al-Bukhari*, "Adab" 27; *Muslim*, "Birr" 15.

43 *al-Bukhari*, "Adab" 36.

44 *Muslim*, "Birr" 8.

45 *Muslim*, "Birr" 14.

46 *Muslim*, "Birr" 41.

47 *al-Bukhari*, "Ashriba," 1; *Muslim*, "Iman," 25.

48 *Abu Dawud*, "Adab" 230.

49 *Abu Dawud*, "Adab" 400.

50 *Abu Dawud*, "Adab" 398.

51 *al-Bukhari*, "Adab" 13.

52 *al-Bukhari*, "Zakah" 1.

53 *al-Bukhari*, "Adab" 11.

54 *al-Bukhari*, "Nikah" 45, "Adab" 62; *Muslim*, "Birr" 5; *Abu Dawud*, "Adab" 40.

55 *Abu Dawud*, "Adab" 133.

56 *Abu Dawud*, "Adab" 146.

57 *al-Bukhari*, "Adab" 44.

58 *Abu Dawud*, "Adab" 175.

59 *al-Bukhari*, "Adab" 105; *Muslim*, "Adab" 5; *at-Tirmidhi*, "Adab" 64.

60 *al-Bukhari*, "Adab" 107; *at-Tirmidhi*, "Adab" 66.

61 *al-Bukhari*, "Adab" 122.

62 *al-Bukhari*, "Adab" 54.

63 *al-Bukhari*, "Adab" 57–58; *Muslim*, "Birr" 7.

64 *Muslim*, "Birr," 18; *Abu Dawud*, "Adab," 40.

65 *Abu Dawud*, "Adab" 102.

66 Said Nursi, *The Letters*, "The Twenty-Second Letter," 2:76–78.

67 *Abu Dawud*, "Adab" 87.

68 *al-Bukhari*, "Adab" 49.

69 Ibn Hanbal, 5:441.

70 *Muslim*, "'Imarah," 8.

71 Ibn Hajar, *al-Isaba fi Tamyiz as-Sahaba*, 1:165.

72 *al-Bukhari*, "Iman," 22, "Adab" 44.

73 *Muslim*, "Fada'il al-Sahabah," 10.

74 Ibn Sa'd, *al-Tabaqat al-Kubra*, 4:70.

75 *Abu Dawud*, "Adab" 346.

76 *Abu Dawud*, "Adab" 345.

77 Abu Shuja' al-Daylami, *Al-Firdaws bi-Ma'thur al-Khitab*, 4:300.

78 *al-Bukhari*, "Hudud" 11; *Muslim*, "Hudud" 2; *at-Tirmidhi*, "Hudud" 9.

CHAPTER 2: HUMANITY: BETWEEN THE HIGHEST OF THE HIGH AND THE LOWEST OF THE LOW

1 *al-Muwatta'*, "Husn al-Khulq" 8; al-Bukhari, *Adab al-Mufrad*, HN:273.

2 at-Tabarani, *Mu'jam al-Kabir*, vol. 8, HN:7502.

3 A. Cressy Morrison, *Man Does Not Stand Alone*, New York, 1945, p. 100.

4 Said Nursi, *The Letters*, (trans.), The Light, New Jersey, 2007, pp. 239–240.

5 Said Nursi, *The Words*, (trans.), The Light, New Jersey, 2005, "The Twenty-Third Word," p. 332.

6 *Hutbe-i Samiye* ("The Sermon of Damascus"), *Risale-i Nur Külliyatı* ("The Risale-i Nur Collection"), Nesil Yayınları, Istanbul, 1996, Vol., 2, p., 1980.

7 Said Nursi, *The Words*, "The Thirtieth Word," 558.

8 Said Nursi, ibid., "The Twelfth Word," 147.

9 See Said Nursi, *The Words*, "The Twentieth Word."

CHAPTER 3: CERTAIN VIRTUES ENCOURAGED IN THE QUR'AN AND THE SUNNA

1 *Abu Dawud*, "Adab" 99.

2 *al-Bukhari*, "Adab" 52; *Muslim*, "Birr" 24.

3 Said Nursi, *The Letters*, "Seeds of the Truth," 2:306.

4 *al-Bukhari*, "Adab" 6.

5 *Abu Dawud*, "Adab" 127, H. No. 4883.

6 *Muslim*, "Birr" 39; *Abu Dawud*, "Adab" 200.

7 *al-Bukhari*, "Da'awat" 2.

8 *Muslim*, "Dhikr" 12.

9 *Abu Dawud*, "Adab" 38.

10 M. Fethullah Gülen, *Key Concepts in the Practice of Sufism: Emerald Hills of the Heart*, (Trans.), Vol., 1, pp., 95–96.

11 Ibn Hanbal, *Musnad*, 1:172; 2:117.

12 *al-Bukhari*, "Adab" 69.

13 *al-Bukhari*, "Adab" 71.

14 *at-Tirmidhi*, "Adab" 41.

15 *al-Bukhari*, "Iman" 37; *Muslim*, "Iman" 1; *Abu Dawud*, "Sunan" 16.

16 *al-Bukhari*, "Iman" 7; *Muslim*, "Iman" 18.

17 *Muslim*, "Sayd" 11; *at-Tirmidhi*, "Diyat" 14.

18 *Muslim*, "Birr" 17.

19 *Abu Dawud*, "Adab" 122.

20 *al-Bukhari* "Tafsir Sura Nun" 68; *Muslim*, "Jannah" 13.

21 Abu Nuʿaym, *Hilyat al-Awliya'*, 7:129.

22 *al-Bukhari*, "Isti'dhan," 15; *Muslim*, "Salam," 5.

23 *al-Bukhari*, "Adab" 61; *Muslim*, "Birr" 38.

24 *al-Bukhari*, "Adhan," 35; *at-Tirmidhi*, "Sifat al-Qiyama," 45..

25 Ibn Hanbal, *Musnad*, 2:383; Ibn Hisham, *as-Sirat an-Nabawiya*, 2:141.

26 *at-Tirmidhi*, *Shama'il*, 78; Ibn Hanbal, *Musnad*, 6:256.

27 *al-Bukhari*, "At'ima," 55; *Muslim*, "Ayman," 10.

28 *al-Bukhari*, "Nafaqat," 1; "Talaq," 25; *Muslim*, "Zuhd," 3.

29 *al-Bukhari*, "Tafsir Sura 9" 12; at-Tirmidhi, "Shama'il" 59–60.

30 M. Fethullah Gülen, *Key Concepts in the Practice of Sufism: Emerald Hills of the Heart*, 1, 76-80.

31 *Muslim*, "Birr," 36.

32 *Abu Dawud*, "Adab" 22.

33 *Abu Dawud*, "Adab" 4.

34 *al-Bukhari*, "Adab" 76; *Muslim*, "Birr" 28.

35 *al-Bukhari*, "Adab" 76.

36 *Abu Dawud*, "Adab" 7.

37 *Abu Dawud*, "Adab" 9.

38 *Abu Dawud*, "Adab" 27.

39 *al-Bukhari*, "Adab" 31, 85; *Muslim*, "Iman" 20.

40 *at-Tirmidhi*, "Zuhd" 11; al-Muvatta', "Husnu'l-Khulq" 3.

41 M. Fethullah Gülen, *Towards the Lost Paradise*, Kaynak, Izmir, 1998, p., 30.

42 *al-Bukhari*, "Adab" 19.

43 *al-Bukhari*, "Adab" 18.
44 *Abu Dawud*, "Adab" 168.
45 *Abu Dawud*, "Adab" 170.
46 *al-Bukhari*, "Adab" 18.
47 *al-Bukhari*, "Adab" 18.
48 *at-Tirmidhi*, "Birr" 15.
49 *Abu Dawud*, "Adab" 446.
50 *Abu Dawud*, "Jihad" 168.
51 *al-Bukhari*, "Anbiya," 54; *Muslim*, "Salam," 38.
52 *Muslim*, "Birr" 35, "Salam" 37.
53 *Abu Dawud*, "Adab," 164, "Jihad," 112; I. Hanbal, 1:404.
54 *al-Bukhari*, "Jihad," 153; *Muslim*, "Salam," 36.
55 *an-Nasa'i*, "Hajj," 114; I, Hanbal, *Musnad*, 1:385.
56 al-Hakim, *al-Mustadrak*, 4:231, 233.
57 *al-Bukhari*, "Bad'u l-Wahy" 7.
58 Ibn Hanbal, *Musnad*, 5:323.
59 *at-Tirmidhi*, "Qiyamah" 60; Ibn Hanbal, *Musnad*, 1:200.
60 *al-Bukhari*, "Adab" 69; *Muslim*, "Birr" 27; *Abu Dawud*, "Adab" 80.
61 *al-Bukhari*, "Adab" 69; *Muslim*, "Iman" 26; *Abu Dawud*, "Sunna" 16; *at-Tirmidhi*, "Iman" 14.
62 *Abu Dawud*, "Adab" 26.
63 *Abu Dawud*, "Adab" 217.
64 *al-Bukhari*, "Adab" 51.
65 *al-Bukhari*, "Adab" 72.
66 *Muslim*, "Iman" 13.
67 *al-Bukhari*, "Adab" 77.
68 *al-Bukhari*, "Adab" 77.
69 *al-Bukhari*, "Adab" 78.
70 *Muslim*, "Hayd" 12.
71 *al-Bukhari*, "Adab" 39; *Abu Dawud*, "Adab" 1.
72 *Muslim*, "Birr" 21; *Abu Dawud*, "Adab" 31.
73 *Abu Dawud*, "Adab" 122.
74 *Abu Dawud*, "Adab" 390.
75 *al-Bukhari*, "Adab" 35.
76 *Muslim*, "Birr" 21.
77 *al-Bukhari*, "Adab" 69.
78 *al-Bukhari*, "Adab" 80.

79 *Muslim*, "Birr" 17.

80 *Abu Dawud*, "Adab" 18.

81 *Abu Dawud*, "Adab" 145.

82 *Abu Dawud*, "Adab" 232; *at-Tirmidhi*, "Adab" 72.

83 *Abu Dawud*, "Adab" 233.

84 *Muslim*, "Birr" 13.

85 *Muslim*, "Birr" 31.

86 *Muslim*, "Birr" 32.

87 *Muslim*, "Birr" 33.

88 *Abu Dawud*, "Adab" 130.

89 *al-Bukhari*, "Buyu'"38; *Muslim*, "Birr" 43; *Abu Dawud*, "Adab" 56.

90 *Abu Dawud*, "Adab" 50.

91 *at-Tirmidhi*, "Birr" 64.

92 *al-Bukhari*, "Adab" 64.

93 *al-Bukhari*, "Adab" 57; *Muslim*, "Birr" 5.

94 *Muslim*, "Birr" 9.

95 Qadi 'Iyad, *as-Shifa' al-Sharif*, 1:78–79.

96 *Abu Dawud*, "Adab" 133.

97 *Abu Dawud*, "Adab" 135.

98 *al-Bukhari*, "Iman" 29; *at-Tirmidhi*, "Birr" 29.

99 *at-Tirmidhi*, "Birr" 31; 5145.

100 *al-Bukhari*, "Adab" 34.

101 *Muslim*, "Fadail al-Nabi" 19; *Abu Dawud*, "Adab" 45.

102 *al-Bukhari*, "Adab" 61; Ibn Maja, "Zuhd" 16.

103 *al-Bukhari*, "Adab" 48.

104 *al-Bukhari*, "Adab" 51.

105 *Abu Dawud*, "Adab" 40.

106 *at-Tirmidhi*, "'Ilm" 15.

107 *al-Bukhari*, "Adab" 28; *Muslim*, "Birr" 40; *Abu Dawud*, "Adab" 378.

108 al-Tabarani, al-*Mu'jam al-Kabir*, 1:232.

109 *al-Bukhari*, "Adab" 31; *Muslim*, "Iman" 20.

110 Ibn Hanbal, *al-Musnad*, 2:33.

111 *Muslim*, "Birr" 40.

112 *al-Bukhari*, "Adab" 29.

113 *Muslim*, "Iman" 19.

114 *al-Bukhari*, "Bad'u'l-Wahy" 3.

115 *al-Bukhari*, "Adab" 24.

[116] *al-Bukhari*, "Adab" 25.

[117] *al-Bukhari*, "Riqaq" 12; *an-Nasa'i*, "Wasaya" 1.

[118] *al-Bukhari*, "Adab" 39.

[119] *al-Bukhari*, "Tafsir, Nun" 1; *Muslim*, "Janna" 13; *at-Tirmidhi*, "Jahannam" 13.

[120] *at-Tirmidhi*, "Birr" 41.

[121] *Abu Dawud*, "Adab" 8.

[122] *al-Bukhari*, "Wasaya" 7; *Muslim*, "Zakah" 29; *Abu Dawud*, "Wasaya" 3.

[123] *al-Bukhari*, "Adab" 31; *Muslim*, "Iman" 20.

[124] *al-Bukhari*, "Adab" 85.

[125] *al-Bukhari*, "Hiba" 11; *at-Tirmidhi*, "Birr" 34.

[126] *at-Tirmidhi*, "Ahkam" 10.

[127] *Abu Dawud*, "Zakah" 114; *an-Nasa'i*, "Zakah" 72.

[128] *at-Tirmidhi*, "Qiyama" 42.

[129] *Abu Dawud*, "Zakah" 84.

[130] *al-Bukhari*, "Adab" 104.

[131] *Muslim*, "Birr" 11.

[132] *Muslim*, "Birr" 11.

[133] See M. Fethullah Gülen, *Pearls of Wisdom*, pp. 77–78.

[134] *al-Bukhari*, "Isti'dhan" 16; *at-Tirmidhi*, "Adab" 59.

[135] *Abu Dawud*, "Adab" 434.

[136] *al-Bukhari*, "Jumu'a" 60; *at-Tirmidhi*, "Adab" 9; *Abu Dawud*, "Adab" 45.

[137] *at-Tirmidhi*, "Adab" 11.

[138] *at-Tirmidhi*, "Adab" 13.

[139] *at-Tirmidhi*, "Adab" 24; *an-Nasa'i*, "Imama" 18.

[140] *al-Bukhari*, "Adab" 60.

[141] *Abu Dawud*, "Adab" 428.

[142] *Abu Dawud*, "Salam" 1; *at-Tirmidhi*, "Isti'dhan" 43.

[143] *Muslim*, "Iman" 15.

[144] *Muslim*, "Salam" 3.

[145] *Muslim*, "Salam" 1.

[146] *Abu Dawud*, "Adab" 423.

[147] *al-Bukhari*, "Isti'dhan" 1.

[148] Said Nursi, *The Letters*, "The Twenty-Second Letter," 2:70–71.

[149] *Muslim*, "Iman" 13.

[150] *Muslim*, "Birr" 34.

[151] *Muslim*, "Birr" 34.

[152] *al-Bukhari*, "Adab" 123; *Muslim*, "Zuhd" 27; *at-Tirmidhi*, "Adab" 3–5.

153 *al-Bukhari*, "Adab" 124.

154 *al-Bukhari*, "Adab" 128; *Muslim*, "Zuhd" 17; *at-Tirmidhi*, "Adab" 7.

CHAPTER 4: VERSES FROM THE QUR'AN AND A COLLECTION OF *HADITH*S CONCERNING GOOD, ISLAMIC MORALS

1 *at-Tirmidhi*, "Zuhd" 2; *Ibn Maja*, "Zuhd" 26.

2 *al-Qurtubi, Tafsir*, in the interpretation of Chapter 7, verse 199.

3 *at-Tirmidhi*, "Qiyama" 53.

4 *at-Tirmidhi*, "Zuhd" 61.

5 *at-Tirmidhi*, "Qiyama" 46.

6 *at-Tirmidhi*, "Birr" 63.

7 *at-Tirmidhi*, "Da'awat" 110.

CHAPTER 5: THE UNEQUALLED CHARACTER OF ALLAH'S MESSENGER

1 *al-Muwatta'*, "Husn al-Khulq" 8; al-Bukhari, *Adab al-Mufrad*, HN:273.

2 *Muslim*, "Salah" 110; *Abu Dawud*, "Salah" 316; *an-Nasa'i*, "Qiyam al-Layl," 2.

3 M. Fethullah Gülen, *Muhammad: The Messenger of Allah – An Analysis of the Prophet's Life*, NJ: Tughra Books, 2009, pp. 283–300.

4 *al-Bukhari*, "Anbiya'" 54; *Muslim*, "Jihad," 36.

5 Ibn Hisham, *Sira*, 4:55; Ibn Kathir, *al-Bidaya wa'n-Nihaya*, 4:344.

6 *Muslim*, "Fara'iz" 4; *al-Bukhari*, "Istiqraz," 11.

7 *Muslim*, "Birr" 22.

8 Ibn Hanbal, *al-Musnad*, 4:395; *Muslim*, "Fada'il an-Nabiyy" 30.

9 *Muslim*, "Hudud" 5; *al-Bukhari*, "Hudud," 28.

10 *al-Bukhari*, "Adhan," 65; *Muslim*, "Salah," 34.

11 *al-Bukhari*, "Adab," 18.

12 *at-Tirmidhi*, "Birr" 16.

13 *al-Bukhari*, "Jana'iz" 45; *Muslim*, "Salah" 177 ("Jana'iz") 5.

14 *Muslim*, "Ayman" 8; Ibn Hanbal, *al-Musnad*, 3:447.

15 *al-Bukhari*, "Bad'u'l-Wahy" 3.

16 *al-Bukhari*, "Anbiya'," 54; *Muslim*, "Salam," 37–38.

17 *Abu Dawud*, "Adab," 164; "Jihad," 112; Ibn Hanbal, *al-Musnad*, 1:404.

18 al-Hakim, *al-Mustadrak*, 4:231, 233.

19 *Muslim*, "Zakah" 44; *al-Bukhari*, "Adab" 95; "Manaqib" 25.

20 *Abu Dawud*, "Adab" 2; *an-Nasa'i*, "Qasama" 24.

21 as-Suyuti, *Al-Khasa'is al-Kubra*, 1:26; Ibn Hajar, *al-Isaba fi Tamyiz as-Sahaba*, 1:566.

22 al-Hakim, *al-Mustadrak,* 3:242.

23 *Muslim*, "Iman" 42; *Ibn Maja*, "Fitan" 1.

24 *al-Bukhari*, "Iman," 22, "Adab" 44.

25 Ibn Kathir, *Al-Bidaya wa'n-Nihaya*, 3:158–159.

26 *al-Bukhari*, "Riqaq" 3.

27 *al-Bukhari*, "Tafsir" 2; *Muslim*, "Talaq" 5.

28 *Muslim*, "Fada'il an-Nabiyy" 24,

29 *al-Bukhari*, "Manaqib" 23; *Muslim*, "Fada'il an-Nabiyy" 11–13.

30 as-Suyuti, *ibid*, 1:123; Muttaqi al-Hindi, *Kanz al-'Ummal*, 7:168.

31 Ibn Kathir, *ibid.*, 6:63.

32 *at-Tirmidhi*, "Birr" 40.

33 Muttaqi al-Hindi, *ibid*, 6:571.

34 Said Nursi, *The Letters* (trans.), p. 455.

35 al-Haythami, *Majma' az-Zawa'id*, 9:21.

36 *al-Bukhari*, "Manaqib al-Ansar"44; Ibn Sa'd, *at-Tabaqat al-Kubra'*, 1:240.

37 *at-Tirmidhi*, "Zuhd" 39.

38 *Ibn Maja*, "At'ima," 30; al-Haythami, *ibid*, 9:20.

39 *al-Bukhari*, "Adab" 61; *Muslim*, "Birr" 38; *Ibn Maja*, "Zuhd" 16.

40 *at-Tirmidhi*, *Shama'il,* 78; Ibn Hanbal, *al-Musnad*, 6:256.

41 *al-Bukhari*, "Riqaq," 18.

42 *Muslim*, "Birr" 17; al-Haythami, *ibid*, 10:325.

43 *at-Tirmidhi*, "Manaqib" 8.

INDEX